THE PROFITS JIGSAW

- *analysing company performance*
- *improving management decisions*
- *boosting employee motivation*

with the INFRA *method*

Flykt, Rydman, Sutton

Chartwell-Bratt
Studentlitteratur

Chartwell-Bratt (Publishing and Training) Limited
ISBN 0-86238-100-2

Studentlitteratur
ISBN 91-44-25941-7

Printed in Sweden by Studentlitteratur, Lund

Contents

Preface

This book is written by two widely experienced Scandinavian consultants who have had the privilege of working on problems with the management and staff of a wide range of businesses. They have also conducted many conferences and seminars and thereby gained an extensive knowledge of the way in which businesses work.

One result of this experience has been the realisation that for many people the presentation of company accounts can be likened to an Impressionist painting. If you do not understand the principles and cannot appreciate all the detail, the significance escapes you. In reality, accounts are not very complicated. By using a limited number of basic figures and presenting them in a form which can be easily understood, a simple but accurate picture of the business can be obtained. Given a simple presentation, each member of the company can understand what is happening, what improvements are needed and what the future may hold. Such understanding has resulted in many dramatic improvements in creativity and in drives to improve results by motivating everyone in the firm.

The main problem for the man in the street when reading published accounts is one of identity. By exhortation, managers try to encourage people to take responsibility for their actions, to make decisions and, by their attitudes and actions, to improve results. However, the company accounts show the work force — from Managing Director to sweeper-up — as an expense; on a par with raw materials, heating oil and protective gloves. The employees are seen as being a cost, a burden which — as with any other cost — has to be reduced if the firm is to prosper.

This attitude and approach will not motivate people. The authors have avoided this trap by focussing on the concept of Added Value.

Added Value (the value of the products or services which are sold, less the cost of purchases of materials and services) is the total outcome of the work done by all members of the company. If the members of the company are seen to be contributing to added value, they can also be seen as participating in the distribution of added value whether they are shopfloor workers, managers, shareholders or the providers of capital.

This book sets out to present a general and simplified picture of the financial process of being in business. After the picture has been painted, it is possible to see with a clearer understanding such concepts as profit, productivity, return on investment, liquidity and gearing — words often used and little understood. The analytical method described in this book is called the INFRA* method.

The aim of this book is to help readers throughout an organisation. Those with no accountancy training but who want to know how their firm is fareing in financial terms will be the main beneficiaries. But there will also be a benefit to those who already understand the figures and who will be in a better position to explain the results to their fellow workers.

---

*INFRA: Institutet för Relationer in Arbetslivet (Institute for Industrial Relations) — the Swedish consultancy organisation responsible for the design of the INFRA method.
INFRA (U.K.) Institute for Financial Ratio Analysis.

Acknowledgements

The joint authors of this book are deeply indebted to many other people without whom it could not have been presented in its present form. To them we extend our most sincere thanks and would like to acknowledge formally the contribution which they have made.

Stella Rydman was responsible for all of the drawings in the parent volume (Arbetsplatsekonomi : Flykt and Rydman : Teknografiska Institutet, 1983). For the present book she carefully revised and, where necessary, re-drew the illustrations which add so much to the book's message.

Siv Flykt, who had checked all of the tables and figures in Arbetsplatsekonomi, repeated this thankless task.

Chapter 3 of the book had to be completely re-written to use an English example. The authors were extremely fortunate in finding a company (Darlington and Simpson Rolling Mills Ltd) which would provide the figures on which the chapter is built. We would like particularly to thank DSRM's Group Director, Commercial — Derrick B. Hale FCA — for permission to use the figures and the Group Manager, Accounting — Fred Garlick FCMA — for actually providing the essential information and advising on its presentation.

The important job of casting an eye over the technical content of the entire book, in the course of which he made many valuable suggestions for amendments and additions, was that of Alan Welsh BSc, MIIM, MCMA, Principal Lecturer in Management Studies of Teesside Polytechnic.

Whatever its shortcomings, for which the authors accept full responsibility, the book would have been much the worse without the contributions of these friends and colleagues and we are deeply grateful to them.

Sven Flykt.
Finn Rydman.
David Sutton.

1 · The Basics of Added Value

Some such figure appears in the annual company report as 'Group profit on ordinary activities for the year before taxation'. This statement should tell the reader something. What does it tell him? Was it a good year? Does it mean anything to someone with no financial knowledge?

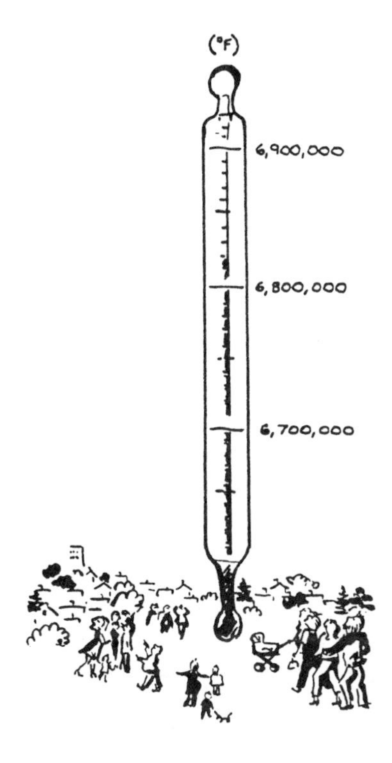

Fig. 1. Unless the information is broken down and presented in a way which you can understand, you cannot recognise its importance.

An annual report is an annual health check when shareholders, directors, lenders of funds, employees, accountants and the public can get an answer to the question — 'How are we doing?' For most people however the statement 'a profit of £70m' is about as informative as saying 'all the population of Scunthorpe took their temperatures at 9 o'clock this morning and the total of all those temperatures was 6,864,000°F.

If you don't know whether to be pleased or sorry when you read your own company's results it can be because of one of two things.

Either —

1. You don't know what is being said. You lack the *knowledge* to understand the message being conveyed. 'Depreciation', 'Interest', 'Tangible Assets' do not convey a picture to you.

Or —

2. You don't have a measure against which to evaluate the figures. Is £70m profit good or bad? You don't have the *understanding* which will help you to put a value on the figures.

Both knowledge and understanding are necessary to give meaning to financial information.

At the root of the problem is the language and terminology which is used. The captain of a yacht realises that he must shorten sail if he is to avoid hitting a rock. He shouts down his megaphone 'Somebody untie that rope on the right.' The crew look at each other. Who is somebody? To the right of the captain or to the right of those facing him? A crewman sees a rope to the right of the mainmast from where he stands. He unties it, the main sail falls on the deck in a heap; there is utter confusion and the yacht drifts on to the rock.

This need not happen. The captain could use his megaphone to shout a message such as 'Crossfield, untie the foresail sheet on the starboard side.' Now there is only one man and one rope. The correct language has been used and the manoeuvre has been successfully completed. The same ideas apply in business. All those involved in making and carrying out decisions — the board, the chairman, the directors, the managers, the supervisors, the union representatives must be able to understand each other if they are to act as a team. They need a comprehensive and common language of finance.

A certain amount of jargon may be necessary but exaggerated jargon with specialist strange and foreign sounding words is undesirable and can be self-defeating. Such terminology is often designed to confuse the uninitiated, to give status to those 'in the know' and incidentally to raise their standing and, possibly, their salaries.

Jargon may be necessary for management when discussing company accounts internally. However, it certainly forms a barrier when discussing financial information with people without financial training or knowledge.

As a result the public in general and the majority of the employees (who have a vital interest in the affairs of the company and whose work determines whether or not the firm will be profitable) cannot take part in discussions about the enterprise and the place it fills in society.

The ability to understand financial statements is needed now more than ever

In a business world which is moving towards increasing decentralisation and participation, more people in every enterprise need to understand and become involved in financial discussions. Terms such as profitability, levels of employment, redundancy, productivity, depreciation and investment are bandied about in both business and politics. Most people do not really understand what these terms mean and how they relate to the firm in which they work. If people cannot understand at that level, they cannot make judgments at the ballot box on a wider political basis.

It is generally agreed that more people need to understand the real nature of business economics. Despite general agreement that there should be greater openness in disclosing financial and business information, the ordinary workman is as much in the dark as ever he was.

A simplified means of describing business activities as seen by the ordinary man is needed — using a language that he can recognise in terms of his personal economy.

The economy of the job is a starting point

A common language to be used by experts and non-experts alike must have a starting point, which can be generally understood and accepted. It seems natural that we should start from the industrial job — the work done day by day by an employee in furtherance of the objectives of his enterprise.

Much has been written about the national economy, the economy of business, the economy of manufacturing and the economy of the firm. Our objective is to develop a model at a level which can be understood by every employee — the economy of the workplace, the economy of the job.

Using the economy of the workplace to improve jobs

Industry and trade exist to produce goods and to perform services. Goods and services are bought and sold. Money, in many forms, changes hands. Work is done and paid for. This is reality. A different way of describing the situation will not change reality. In whatever way it is described, reality will, in the short term, remain the same. What is equally real is that people make decisions and act on those decisions on the basis of their understanding of what is happening in reality. This understanding is largely determined by how events are described.

The only justification for using a new method to describe the operation of an enterprise is that it should increase knowledge and understanding. The more people who can understand what is happening, the more there are who can take an intelligent part in the operation of the firm and, by their ideas, suggestions and enthusiasm affect its future. People working in the firm will be able to understand each other and to understand the contribution made by each member of the firm. Confusion about information and in discussion will be reduced. Conflict, based on misunderstanding, will diminish. Ideas, opinions and suggestions will be drawn from a wider range of people. The way in which employees, departments and entire organisations perform will be influenced in a positive and constructive way. Each individual job will have more meaning and will be performed more effectively. Practical experience of improvements of this kind have been achieved in Scandinavia using the methods described in this book.

'Approximately' is sometimes better than 'accurately but incomprehensible'

The economy of a business is complicated. It cannot be fully described accurately and simply. To all but the trained accountant the detailed, accurate financial description is incomprehensible. A descriptive method has to be balanced between precision and intelligibility. Precision which cannot be understood has no value. The desired solution is to present only the essentiais; using a tool that shows the present position and indicating the direction in which the business must go.

An orienteer who tries to gain an advantage by using a satellite navigation system, which he does not understand and cannot read, is likely to find himself finishing behind other competitors who have trusted in an ordinary compass giving them only a general guide to direction.

Fig. 2. A simple but easily understood instrument is better than a technically advanced system which the user does not understand.

A descriptive method has been chosen based on the understanding that money is needed to create jobs. The chosen model is one of cash flow because of the importance of controlling the flow of receipts and disbursments if the company is not to go into liquidation.

See the business as a human body. The buildings, machinery, equipment and employees are the muscles. In order to work, the muscles need a flow of blood. Cash flow is the blood stream of the business enabling the muscles to carry out the jobs which fulfil the tasks. If the stream of blood/cash dries up, the body/business ceases to work and the result is death/liquidation. A world champion wrestler would lose to a second-rate opponent if he had lost a lot of blood. He would be lifeless and have to concede the bout. In the same way, many firms reach a crisis not because the machinery or equipment has failed, but because the cash has run out.

Increased efficiency and higher productivity is not just a question of improved production resulting in increased profit. It is also a question of improving the flow of cash so that jobs can be financed.

By considering our own money affairs we can learn something about the way a business works

Jobs are the means whereby a business achieves its objectives. Most people want a job — just as they want a place in which to live. We know we can get our own place in which to live either by renting from someone else or by buying our own flat or house. We also know that accommodation is expensive and we know that house purchase can be financed — usually by saving part of the purchase price and borrowing the rest; on a loan or a mortgage.

It is amazing that, although most people understand the intricacies of house purchase, or of hire purchase, very few understand how their jobs are financed. Having a job is as important as having a place in which to live. In fact, to most of us, it is more important: without a job we cannot afford the house. The ways in which house purchase and job creation are financed are remarkably similar and it is no more difficult to understand one than the other.

A job involves finance of the same dimensions as a house purchase — neither the petty cash for buying a bar of chocolate nor the millions of pounds needed to launch a satellite. There is, therefore, a case for looking at business finance on a cost/income per job basis, because the ordinary person can comprehend the sums of money which are involved. To pursue the house/job comparison let us look at the way in which accommodation is financed.

Renting a place of one's own

Take a simple example — tenancy of an apartment of 1400 square feet, no down payment or key money (no need to invest capital) and an ordinary tenancy agreement — payment monthly in advance and certain conditions regarding repairs etc. You agree on the rent and move in. Then you receive your first demand for rent.

Rent: April 1985 £218.00

The calculation behind this sum of £218 is not shown on the invoice. It is a figure you have accepted, based on calculations made by the landlord who knows the costs (costs of finance, wages, materials, office costs) which he has incurred in purchasing the property, making it suitable for occupation and maintaining it in good order in accordance with various statutory orders (fire, sanitation, preservation orders, security of the structure etc.) and the requirements of the tenants. All these costs are included in the calculation of the rent and hidden from the tenant.

It is not easy to get accurate analyses of finance for lettings but a journalist's example from April 1982 reads as follows:

A family owns two houses built in 1930. Each house has been modernised and has a flat on each of the six floors. The rental includes lifts, maintained gardens, cleaning, central heating and a permanent janitor. The annual rent for each flat has been fixed at a figure of £1.87 per sq. ft. based on the following costs.

Annual Costs of running a 1,400 sq. ft. flat

Maintenance	£490	=	£.35 per sq. ft.
Ground Rent	£ 56	=	£.04 per sq. ft.
Wages and Salaries	£238	=	£.17 per sq. ft.
Cleaning	£ 56	=	£.04 per sq. ft.
Heating	£602	=	£.43 per sq. ft.
Water	£ 48	=	£.03 per sq. ft.
Electricity	£154	=	£.11 per sq. ft.
Insurance	£ 42	=	£.03 per sq. ft.
Others	£ 14	=	£.01 per sq. ft.
Interest and depreciation	£462	=	£.33 per sq. ft.
Profit	£462	=	£.33 per sq. ft.
			£1.87 per sq. ft.

Rent is therefore £1.87 per sq. ft. = £2,618 per annum.*

A description of the total financial situation for the two houses would be quite complicated. The explanation of the rental charged which has been decided upon is simple if two points can be agreed:

(1) How to illustrate the figures. In this case a simple table.

(2) The choice of an acceptable and easily understood measure for purposes of comparison. In this case £ per sq. ft.

Cost/Income per hour is the key

In his description of the economics of renting property, the journalist chose £s per sq. ft. as the basis for his description. His purpose was to begin with an acceptable and understandable unit of measurement. The number of square feet you rent or buy is a sensible measure for property. With the additional advantage that everyone knows what you mean and can make comparisons with their present accommodation and any other which is on offer.

*Overall the houses gave the owners a 7% return on their capital. Real estate companies were, in 1982, looking for an immediate 9% on invested capital and much of their property realised 25%. There are also examples of houses bought in the 1920s which return hundreds of per cent on the original investment. The idea of what is a 'fair return' or 'the right return' is irrelevant in practice. Reality is 'what rent is asked for and paid?'

The INFRA method of describing business operations is to use the 'working hour' as a base for calculation. Most people see their job as occupying so many hours per week for so many weeks per year in return for which they get a wage or salary. In fact many jobs have the wage expressed as a rate per hour and work is frequently charged for by repairers of motor cars or house property at an hourly rate. The working hour is also a useful means of comparison between large and small firms, between industry and commerce, between manufacturing and service industries and so on. Equally important, it reduces figures for large organisations to a size which can easily be grasped.

Jobs cost money

As with houses, the cost of providing a job can spread over a wide scale but falls within the same range. The capital cost of providing a job usually falls between £10,000 and £100,000. It is also possible to 'buy' or 'rent' a job — just as you can buy or rent accommodation. If you run your own business you have bought, or invested in, your own job. If you are in employment someone else 'owns' the job and you have a Contract of Employment which defines the conditions under which you have agreed to be employed.

Owning your own job

A simple example can demonstrate the costs of owning your own job and show the need for planning and budgeting if you are to be successful.

Imagine that a young man, with some training as a baker, inherits an old family recipe for spiced bread and decides to set up his own business, making a living out of baking and selling 'Lancashire Spiced Bread' to shops and restaurants. He is convinced that the quality and the distinctive flavour will make the bread sell well at a higher than usual price.

He calculates that it will cost him about £30,000 to buy baking equipment. If he can find this sum of money plus, say, £5,000 for working capital (to buy materials, pay start-up costs, set up a book-keeping system and give him something to live on until the cash starts to flow in) he can set himself up in business — owning his own job.

He is then faced with the problem of what to charge and what profit he can expect to show. By pricing the ingredients he discovers that raw material for one of his loaves will cost 12p. He will be able to produce about 25 loaves per hour working on his own in the bakery. Spiced bread sells for between 70p and 80p per loaf. If he charges 70p per loaf he will have an income (turnover) of £17.50 per hour. The idea shows promise.

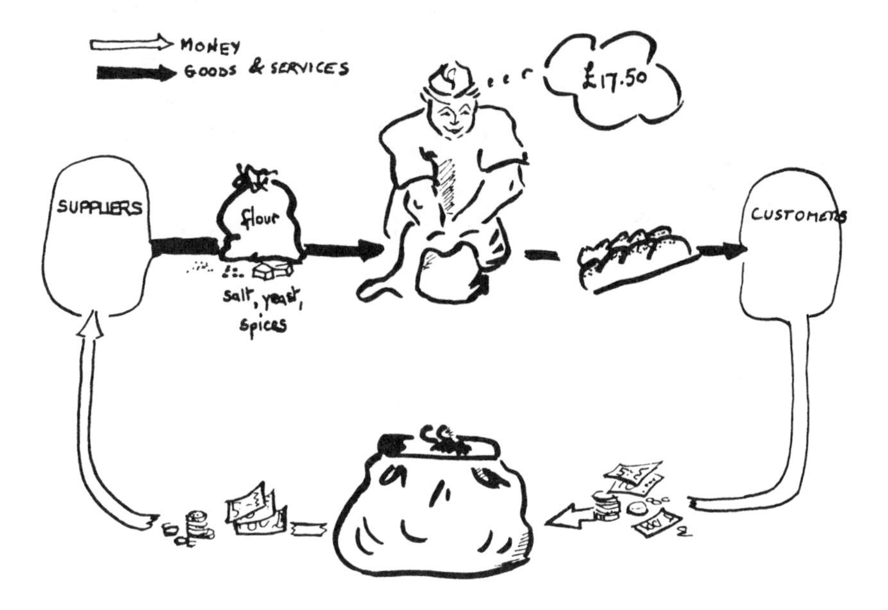

Fig. 3 Adding value means creating value for which customers are willing to pay. To the proprietors added value is what is left in the till after deducting what you pay your suppliers from what your customers pay you.

Added Value is the key to understanding the finances of a business

Our hero's idea is that people will be willing to pay 70p for one of his loaves. Their alternative is to pay 12p for the material and bake the spiced bread themselves. The difference (58p) is what he will be paid by the customer for carrying out the complete baking process from buying the raw materials to delivering loaves of spiced bread to their premises.

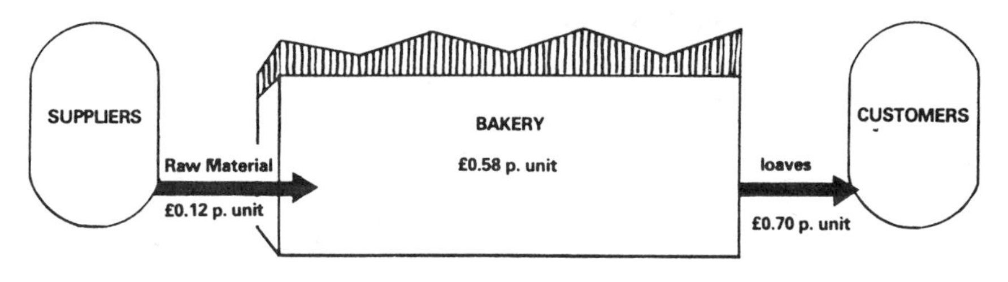

All of the 58p for each loaf does not go to the baker. Some is absorbed by his costs of running the business. He has to pay wages, the bank wants interest on money borrowed, he has to pay rent, rates, taxes. There are many 'interested parties'.

Using the same sort of layout as that used for the housing example we can set up a simple table.

Added Value

Line	Legend	£ per hour	
1.	Invoiced sales	17.50	
2.	Materials		?
3.	Production costs		?
4.	Added value	?	
5.	Wages and salaries		?
6.	NHIC		?
7.	Corporate taxes — Local (rates) and national		?
8.	Interest		?
9.	Dividends		?
10.	To interested parties	?	
11.	Left in business (4-10)	?	

Let us now replace the question marks by the estimated figures.

Raw materials cost money

Flour, milk, butter, sugar, yeast, packing materials, the secret spices must all be bought. These are the raw materials. If the cost of materials for each loaf is 12p, the cost of material used each hour is 25 loaves × 12p = £3.00. The baker must sell bread to the value of £3.00 each hour to pay for his purchases of raw materials, if he produces at the 25 loaves per hour rate.

The act of producing costs money

The services purchased to enable him to produce can be built up to an annual figure. Rent, say, £3,000 per year. Running costs (electricity, water, transportation etc.) say, £2,500 per year. Insurance, audit fees, telephone, stationery, say, £3,740 per year.

In addition to materials we have, therefore, production costs of £3,000 plus £2,500 plus £3,740 — a total of £9,240 per year.

To calculate a cost per hour the total cost must be divided between the working hours for the year. The baker will not be able to open every day. Making allowance for statutory holidays, his own vacation, possible lost time through sickness, breakdown, failure of supplies etc., let us assume a working year of 210 days — 1680 hours.

By dividing £9,240 by 1680 working hours he arrives at a production services cost of £5.50 per hour. In making 25 loaves per hour he will spend £3 on materials and his cost per hour for materials and production services will be £3 plus £5.50 = £8.50.

Money costs money

It is not very often that a person wanting to open his own small bakery has £35,000 in cash. You have to do as you would when buying yourself a home. Put in what you have (like the deposit on a house) and go to the bank to borrow the remainder.

Let us assume that our young baker empties his bank account and sells his car and in that way raises £12,500. The bank lends him £22,500 at 17% interest to be paid back over 5 years.

Henceforth the bank will debit his account with interest of £956 each quarter (£3,825 per annum) — a cost of £2.30 per hour on his 1,680 hour working year. The cost per loaf of materials, production services and bank interest is now £8.50 plus £2.30 = £10.80 per hour.

Amortisation

In the same way that a building society asks for repayment of the capital sum advanced in a mortgage, the bank asks for repayment of the capital sum of £22,500 it has loaned to start tne business. The bank's quarterly debit will include amortisation (repayment of capital) as a sum of £375.00, the equivalent of £1,500 per year and 90p per working hour. The total cost is now £10.80 plus 90p = £11.70 per working hour.

Personal income

The baker hopes to be left with a profit at the end of the year but, to keep himself week by week, he has to pay himself something. Let us say he pays himself £5 per hour plus a further £1 for NHI charges, third party insurance, insurance to provide an income if he is ill etc. A total of £6 per hour brings his necessary level of earnings to £17.70 per working hour.

The business or the baker as an individual will have to pay taxes

His accountant helps him to forecast that, if things go as he plans, his liability for rates and tax arrives at £1,500 per annum. This represents 90p per hour which added to £17.70 gives a total cost of £18.60 per hour.

We are already above the estimated income of £17.50 per hour from 25 loaves at 70p each. What will the loaves really cost?

What of the future?

The machinery in a bakery wears out sooner or later. The machinery may not actually break down or become impossible to use. Any veteran car owner will tell you that with regular repair and constant maintenance an old machine can be kept going indefinitely. The bakery machinery does, however — like a veteran car — become old-fashioned. New machines, like new cars, are likely to be cheaper to run, easier to use, faster running and cheaper to maintain, and also have added ancillaries. An old machine is competed out of business, rather than worn out.

Let us assume that our baker will need new equipment after ten years. The problem is more complicated than straightforward replacement at the same price — the new equipment will cost more than £30,000. Let us assume a price rise of 10% each year for the ten years as a result of inflation and technical improvements. We arrive at a figure of £78,000 — a lot of saving to do. It is not likely that the baker will either want or be able to save £78,000 over ten years and pay for the new machinery in cash. He borrowed most of the money the first time and will want to borrow again, although the bank will expect him to put down a reasonable part of the purchase price himself. If he can save £200 per month for ten years, with compound interest he will have £38,400 for a down payment on his new machinery. £200 per month (£2,400 per year) means putting on one side £1.40 per working hour.

Our final conclusion is that if he is to cover every cost and be in a position to keep his plant up to date the baker needs a sales income of £18.60 plus £1.40 = £20 per working hour.

How good are the loaves of bread?

If his production is restricted to 25 loaves per hour and his costs are as outlined above, the baker must charge 80p per loaf in order to stay in business. Let us hope that his Lancashire spiced bread is so distinctive and nutritious that he will be able to persuade customers to pay that price.

We can now complete our table summarising the every day economics of this bakery business.

Line	Legend	£ per hour	
1.	Invoiced sales (25 at 80p.)	20.00	
2.	Materials		3.00
3.	Production costs		5.50
		8.50	
4.	Added value	11.50	
5.	Personal income		5.00
6.	NHIC etc.		1.00
7.	Taxes and rates		90
8.	Interest		2.30
9.	Dividends		Nil
10.	To interested parties	9.20	
11.	Left in business	2.30	
Breakdown of line 11.	Amortisation	0.90	
	Future investment	1.40	

From the customer's point of view the system looks like this — each loaf costs 80p and is made from materials costing 12p.

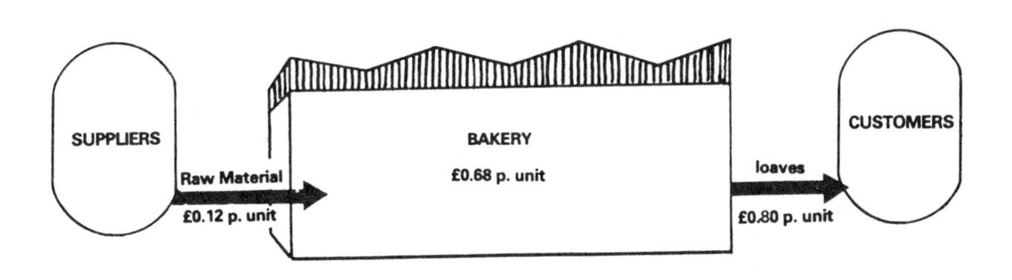

From the baker's point of view the business appears as a manufacturing system in which for every hour worked he produces 25 loaves with a total value of £20, against which he has to pay out £3 for materials and £5.50 for production services — the balance (added value) being available for distribution to the participants in the business.

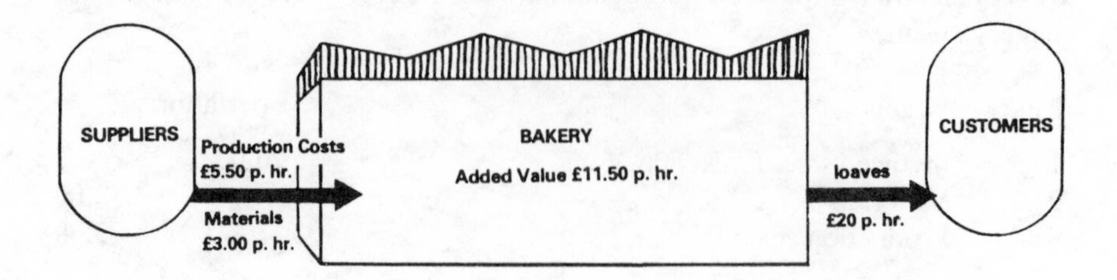

So long as the customers are willing to pay 80p per loaf the business will continue to operate and the baker will keep himself in a job.

The income the baker gets from his customers must be enough to meet the material costs, the production costs and an added value sufficient to satisfy all the interested parties. Otherwise he will use up all his capital and sooner or later his 'own' job will disappear.

This example can be summed up by saying:

If you:

(a) buy (invest in) a job of your own and can raise the sum of £35,000

(b) accept that you will need renewed investment in ten years

(c) want a wage of £5 per working hour (£8,400 per year)

you will have to provide a product or service which will generate an added value of £11.50 per working hour.

Being an employee

The parallel between being employed and renting a house or flat in which to live has been established. An ordinary agreement to be an employee does not need capital investment. You agree on a wage, accept the working conditions and go to work.

Your first pay-check arrives and might look like this:

Hours worked	40 at £4 per hour	£160.00
Deductions		£ 56.00
Net pay		£104.00

The calculations on which the figure of £4 per hour are based are not shown on the pay-cheque. These facts are known only to the employer or possibly shared between the employer and the union negotiator. In making these calculations the cost of capital, production costs, administration costs, selling costs, depreciation, reserves for future investment and many other items are taken into account, but these figures are not revealed to the employee.

An example from a big company

A look at the finances of a large British company in 1984 shows that a great deal of money was required for the cash in hand and the purchase of machinery and equipment, raw materials, consumable supplies, and all the other items to keep the company in operation.

At the end of the year the capital value of the company (what it was worth) was £5,598,000. The company employed 425 people working a total of 714,000 hours in the year. Each job, therefore, represented an investment of $\frac{£5598000}{425}$ = £13,171. Total sales were £14,080,000: raw materials cost £6,322,100 and the total production costs were £1,878,800. Added value was £5,879,100 for the year = £8.23 per working hour.

Was £8.23 per hour enough? How was the money used? Now compare some of these figures with those for the bakery.

For one man's job in the bakery the baker had to raise £35,000 in capital — £30,000 in bakery equipment and £5,000 in working capital. It is interesting, without necessarily drawing conclusions, to compare the figures of the large corporation with those of our mythical one-man firm.

The bakery is modern and very capital intensive. The result: an investment of £35,000 per job. Work in the big firm is on older, partly depreciated machinery and there is not so much capital employed for each job; as is shown by the capital per job figure of £13,171.

For each hour worked the big firm has lower production costs (£2.65 against £5.50) but the added value per hour is only £8.23 against the baker's £11.50 because of the much higher cost per hour of materials. For its size, the big company has low borrowings — the banks only participate to the extent of 23p per hour; the bakery figure is £2.30.

Perhaps the most important key figure is the money left in the business; only £1.64 per working hour in the big firm and £2.30 per working hour in the bakery. Are jobs in danger in the big firm? Has the baker been too ambitious in his target for savings? We may be able to form a better opinion as we get further into this book. What we can agree upon is that the future of the business and of the jobs in it depend upon two things.

1. The amount of added value which the company achieves.
2. The way in which this added value is distributed.

Some of the outlays demanded from a company are determined without the firm having control over their level or their frequency. Banks ask for payment at agreed rates of interest and repayment. Taxes are demanded on a legally approved scale. Agreements exist covering employees' wages. In addition to all of these the added value figure must allow for savings for future investment. Jobs rarely vanish because of demands for high salaries and wages. Companies decline because the value added is not sufficient to cover the *total* demands of *all* the interested parties.

The Concept of Added Value

Workplaces can look very different; but they are usually quite tangible. There is a machine to operate, a bench to work on or a desk to sit at. Materials on which work has to be done (castings, components, documents) flow through the workplace. The job consists of doing something to these materials so that a changed product can be passed on to the next work station or even to the customer. If the job has not enhanced the material — 'added value' to it — the work has been wasted.

The same rules apply to international corporations and to our one-man bakery. The purpose of the jobs in the firm is to add value to the materials so that the customer is willing to pay more than the price of the raw material and, in this way, recompense the firm for the work which it has done.

Many companies add value without processing the materials. A customer is willing to pay for having goods stored, transported or put on display for him to choose from. We pay a higher price per kg. for our sugar for the advantage of getting it in our local Tesco or Spar instead of having to collect it in 50 kg sacks from the Tate & Lyle refinery. Value has been added by packing, transportation and presentation.

An agglomeration of workplaces

An enlarged aerial photograph gives an accurate picture of a stretch of land. But this photograph could not be used as a map for finding one's way. There is too much detail and the important features are not emphasised. The job of the cartographer is to remove unnecessary detail, emphasise the main features such as roads, buildings, rivers and hills and, by using a simple sign language, to help us to recognise the things we see on our journey. The map is a simplified and identifiable version of the landscape, not just a large- or small-scale version of the photograph. As a result it is easier to understand and to use.

What goes on day by day in a large company appears, to the outsider, to be an unorganised confusion of people, materials, goods, documents, vehicles, machines and so on. To those with the knowledge it is a complex, organised collection of workplaces with a financial pattern which decides what shall be done — when, how and by whom. Any attempt to describe this welter of activities in detail would be quite incomprehensible. Like the cartographer, the accountant seeks to emphasise the basic (financial) pattern, simplify the picture by viewing everything in money terms and bring out the important information.

A cycle of goods, services and money

The first stage of building our model is easily recognised as being a copy of the bakery model. By recognising that the goods go through three stages in the factory: *raw material stock* before use, *work in progress* (during which the raw materials go through the processes needed to turn them into the final product) and *finished goods* ready for despatch; we start to build the model.

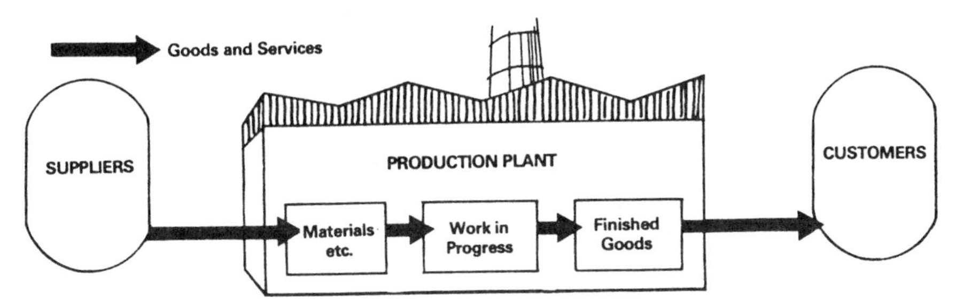

To carry out its work a business needs employees. It also needs the power, the equipment, the premises (works, offices, warehouses etc.) and all the small items — telephone, stationery etc. All these make up the production costs. It also has to *invest in fixed assets* (plant and machinery).

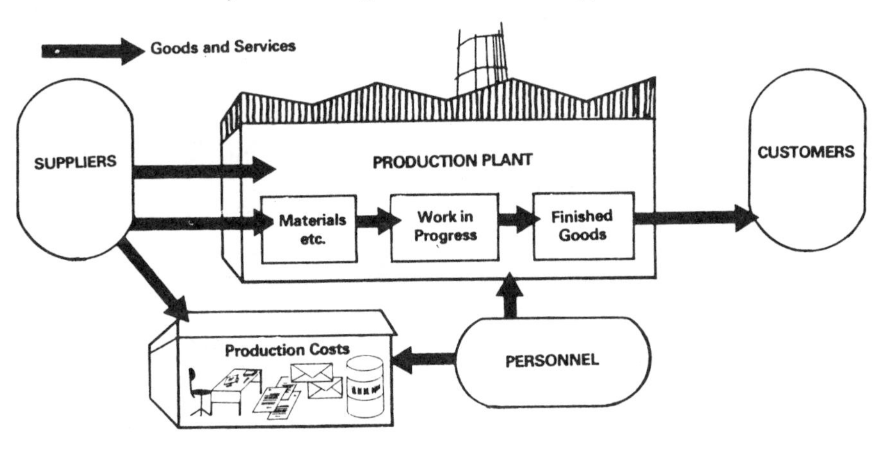

Raw materials, employees, production costs and assets cost *money.* The money to run the company comes from *customers* who pay for the goods which are supplied. If a customer goes into liquidation before he has paid what he owes the firm may lose all or part of that debt. This is called *bad debts.*

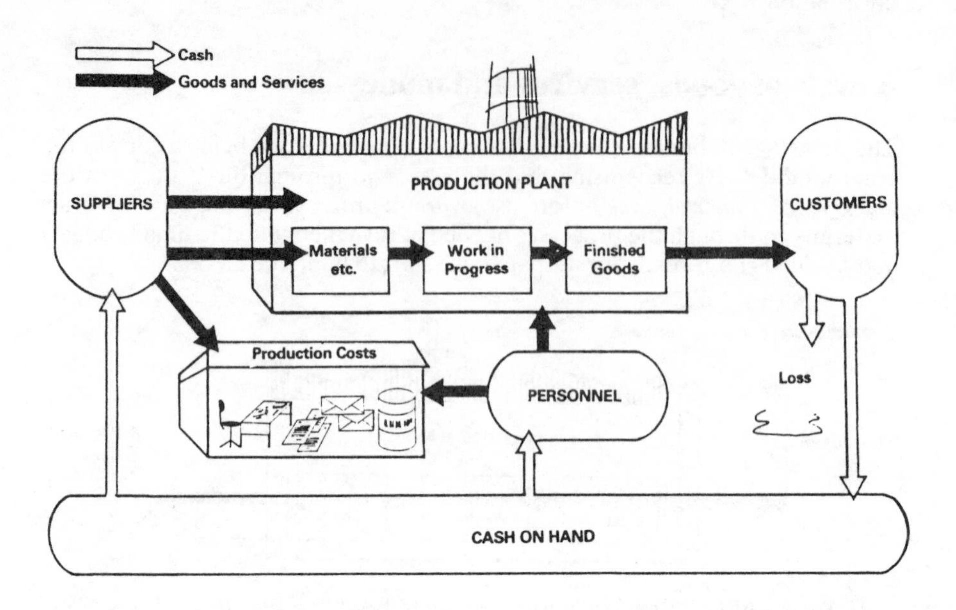

To start a business, capital is needed — *working capital* in the form of *cash* to pay for materials, wages and services. This working capital is needed to set the company in operation before the first goods or services are sold to the customer.

Fixed capital is also needed in the form of land, buildings, plant and machinery to form the working environment.

There are different ways of raising this capital. One way is by selling shares in the firm. This makes the shareholders the owners of the firm; in return for which they will be paid dividends out of future profits.

Some of the initial capital can be borrowed — usually from a bank. The bank will be paid for the money it has lent by charging interest and will require the loan to be repaid (amortised) over a specified period of time.

Society also has claims on the company — the company share of its employees' National Health Insurance *contributions,* local *rates* and *taxes* on profits. In return there are sometimes government *grants or subsidies* — some of which have to pay *interest* and *amortisation* like a bank loan.

Including all of these we get a complete model of the business.

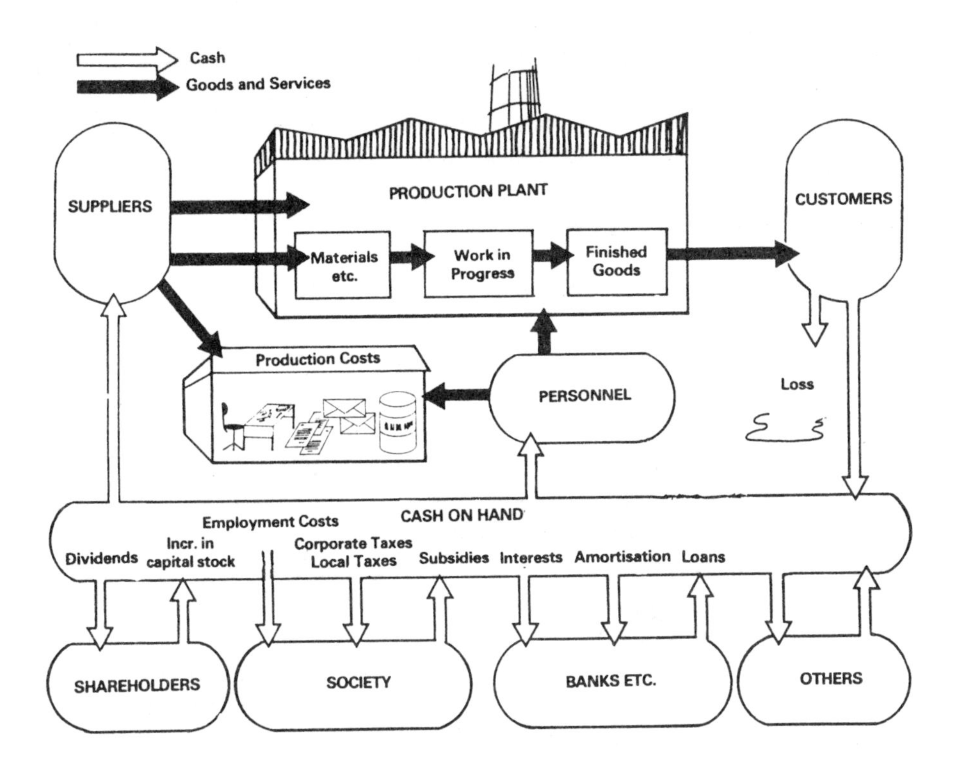

Now we can see the whole cycle of goods, services and money. The company buys goods and services, turns them into finished goods or a more advanced service (by adding value) and sells the goods or services to its customers. Some of the income from the customer is used to make payments in cash or through the bank by cheques or drafts to pay for the company's purchases as indicated by the arrows in the model. If the money received from the customer is not enough to pay these outgoings someone (the owners, the government, the banks or someone else) must provide the balance otherwise the company goes into liquidation.

Who participates in the company?

A great many people participate in the company's activities. The suppliers have to supply materials and, in return, require to be paid. The customers pay for the goods or services they receive according to the quality of the goods or service. Some of the participants share directly in the added value part of the income — they are the employees, the owners (shareholders), the government (local and central) and the lenders of money (usually banks).

WHO PARTICIPATES?

Participants	Contribution	Claims
Customers	Payment for finished goods and services	Goods and services which satisfy them
Suppliers	Goods and services needed in the conversion process to which value is added	Payment for goods and services
Employees	Work Skills Ideas	Salary Working environment Job satisfaction Personal development
Society	Roads, schools, public services	Corporate taxes NHI contributions Cost of environmental protection Rates and local taxes
Banks & finance houses	Loans	Amortisation Interest
Owners (shareholders)	Starting capital Additional (incremental) capital	Preservation of value of capital Dividends

All of the 'contributions' are essential if the jobs in the company are to continue and develop. A shortfall in any 'contribution' will create problems. If the company cannot meet the requirements of any of the participants, that 'contribution' will decrease or disappear. If, for instance, the owners, the employees or society take too big a share of the added value the future of the firm and its employees' jobs may be at risk. There must always be a balance between participants' contributions and their claims. The customer does not pay in order to satisfy all the other participants — he pays to have his own needs satisfied. In times of prosperity for the company when customers are willing to buy in large quantities or at high prices the increased added value will leave more for the other participants to share. When the firm is trading unsuccessfully there will be less in the added value pot to be shared between the other participants.

2 · What do the figures mean?

We start by building a model of the company's performance from the published accounts. A typical set of accounts as summarised in the Profit and Loss Account and the Balance Sheet could be as follows. (The figures in brackets will be used later when analysing the accounts by the INFRA method.):

Profit and Loss Account 19X1

		£000s	
Turnover		4,660	(1)
Cost of sales		4,340*	*
Profit before depreciation		320	(26)
Depreciation		− 60	(27)
		260	(28)
Income from investments	10		
Less Interest charges	−60		
Balance of Interest charges		− 50	(8)
Profit before tax		210	(29)
Taxation		− 30	(30)
Profit after tax		180	(31)
Proposed dividend		− 20	(9)
Profit retained		160	

*Comprising:		
Materials	2,110	(2)
Wages & Salaries	1,320	(5)
Employment costs	270	(6)
Production costs	640	(3)
	4,340	

Balance Sheet 19X1

	31.12.19X1 £000s	31.12.19X0 £000s	Change £000s	
Fixed assets	1,240	1,160	+ 80	(18)
less depreciation	−500	−440	− 60	(27)
	740	720	+ 20	
Current Assets				
Stocks	150	120	+ 30	(21)
Trade debtors	620	510	+110	(19)
Cash at bank and in hand	10	30	− 20	(25)
Short term investments	40	30	+ 10	(22)
	820	690	+130	
Current Liabilities				
Trade creditors	400	310	+ 90	(12)
Current account	100	100	0	
Other current liabilities	90	90	0	
Proposed Dividend	20	20	0	(9)
Taxation Provision	30	30	0	
	640	550	+ 90	
Net current assets	180	140	+ 40	
Total assets less current liabilities	920	860	+ 60	
Long term loans	−640	−740	−100	(23)
	280	120	+160	
Capital and reserves				
Called up share capital	100	100	0	
Profit and loss account	180	20	+160	
	280	120	+160	

From these figures how can we find added value, allocations between interested parties, the amount left in the business and other information which interests us? To do so we will have to translate the figures in the annual accounts by using the INFRA method.

Where does the money come from and where does it go?

The figures quoted are typical of those from any company. They follow in their presentation 'good financial practice'. Let us call this firm 'Big Baker Ltd.' and see how the figures can be entered in a form to comply with the INFRA model. During the year 19X1 Big Baker Ltd. invoiced sales to the value of £4,660,000 and bought raw materials, packing and other materials value £2,110,000. Office supplies, travel, telephone and other production costs amounted to £640,000. The company's 150 employees together performed 240,000 hours of work in the course of the year. By dividing the total cash sum in any category by 240,000 we get the value in £s per hour.

We will build up the INFRA table

Where Does the Money Come From and Where Does It Go?

Line		Total £000s	£s/hour
1.	Invoiced Sales	4,660	19.42
2.	Materials etc.	−2,110	− 8.79
3.	Production Costs	− 640	− 2.67
4.	Added Value	=1,910	= 7.96

In the model these figures are shown as:

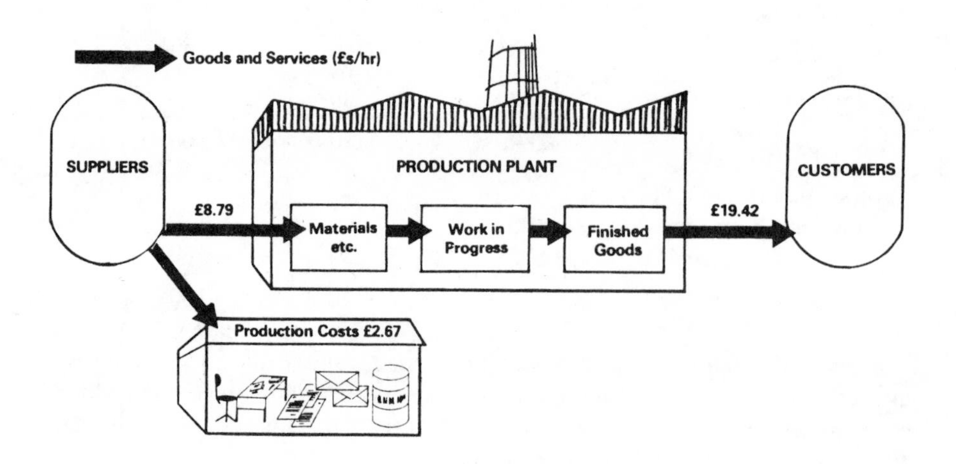

At this stage, the only interested parties who have had their share are the customers who have received their goods and the suppliers who have been paid or are owed for what they have provided. It remains for the £7.96 per hour added value to be divided between the remaining interested parties.

Where Does the Money Come From and Where Does It Go?

Line	Total £000s	£s/hour
1. Invoiced Sales	4,660	19.42
2. Materials etc.	−2,110	8.79
3. Production Costs	− 640	2.67
4. Value Added	1,910	7.96
DISTRIBUTION		
5. To Personnel: wages and salaries	1,320	5.50
6. To Society: Employment costs	+ 270	1.13
7. To Society: Taxes	+ 30	0.13
8. Bank Interest	+ 50	0.21
9. To Shareholders: Dividends	+ 20	0.08
10. Total to Interested Parties	1,690	7.04
11. Left in business (1,910 — 1,690)	= 220	0.92

In the model, it looks like this:

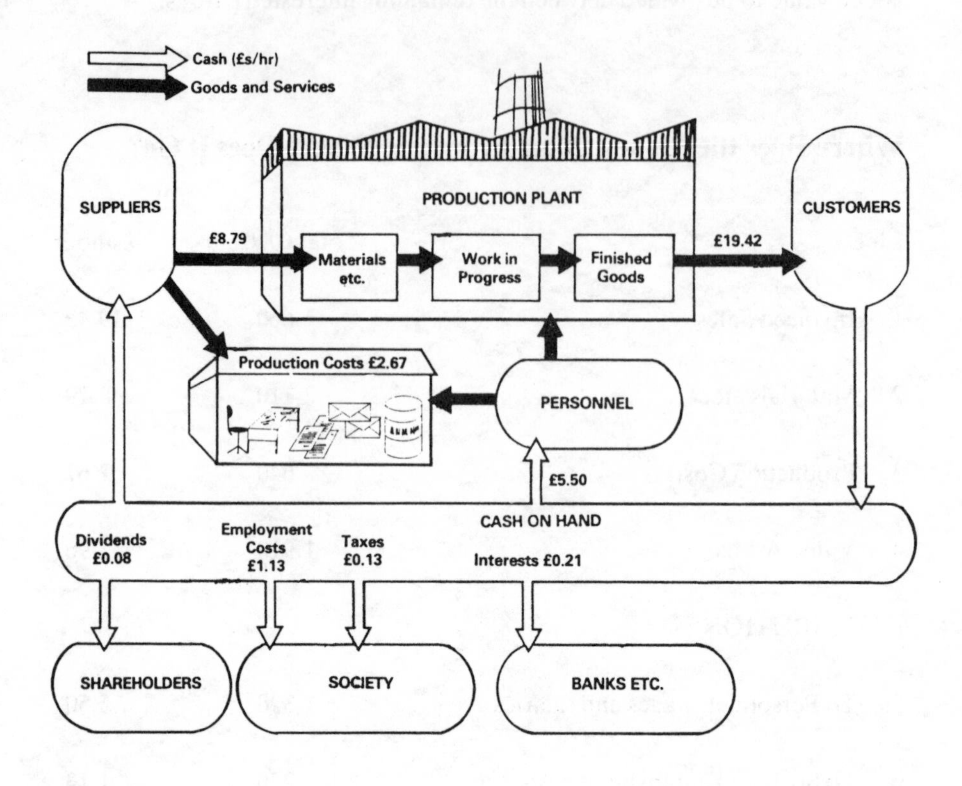

External Financing

After distributing to the interested parties their share of the added value, £220,000 is left in the business. Companies borrow money to finance their business and Big Baker Ltd. had on 1st January borrowed £740,000 from the bank which had reduced to £640,000 by 31st December. But debts in the form of unpaid invoices (*Creditors*) have increased by £90,000 (£0.38 p hr) — the same effect on cash flow as borrowing £90,000 from the bank.

By adding this increase in Creditors to the £220,000 we have the sum of £310,000 or £1.30 per hour at our disposal to run the business.

How the money was used

To complete our analysis and the INFRA model we must take into account several other things that have happened during the year.

- A new electric oven has been bought for £65,000. The firm has also bought a new lorry for £7,000 and has spent £8,000 on office furniture. A total of new *acquisitions* to the value of £80,000.

- Customers do not, of course, pay as soon as the goods are delivered. Payment of goods is usually asked for within 28 days of the date of the invoice. There are always unpaid customers' invoices. On 1st January the sum outstanding was £510,000. By 31st December this sum had risen to £620,000 — an increase during the year of £110,000 in *Debtors*.

- At stocktaking at the end of the previous year the raw materials, packing materials etc. in stock were valued at £120,000. By the end of the year the value of the goods in stock had risen to £150,000 — an increase in *Inventory and Work in Progress* of £30,000. In other words, in addition to the goods used during the year, further goods to the value of £30,000 had been bought.

- In order to pay for goods bought, Big Baker has borrowed from the bank over the year. These loans have been *amortised* over the years and during the year: £100,000 was committed in this way.

- £10,000 has been borrowed by an associated firm which deals in confectionery packaging and is included in *short-term investments*.

The total of all these expenditures is £330,000 — £1.38 per hour — all of this used up inside the company.

Cash in Hand

We can now complete the table. There was £310,000 available and £330,000 was spent. The excess of £20,000 was taken from *cash in hand* — a matter of 8p per hour.

The completed table and the working model are on the following pages. The numbers in brackets in the model which opened this chapter correspond to the line numbers in the table. The future of the company and the jobs which it provides depend upon there always being money available — not only money for current expenses for materials, overheads and wages, but also money for the future — to make purchases and to provide reserves for trading.

Fig. 4. The only way to keep jobs safe is always to have cash available.

Where Does the Money Come From and Where Does It Go?

LINE	ADDED VALUE		£000	£/Hr	LINE
1	Invoiced Sales	+	4,660	19.42	1
2	Materials etc.	−	2,110	8.79	2
3	Production Costs	−	640	2.67	3
4	Added Value	=	1,910	7.96	4
	TO PARTICIPANTS:				
5	To Personnel: Wages and Salaries	+	1,320	5.50	5
6	To Society: Employment Costs	+	270	1.13	6
7	Corporate Taxes	+	30	0.13	7
8	To Banks etc: Interests	+	50	0.21	8
9	To Shareholders: Dividends	+	20	0.08	9
10	Total to Interested Parties	=	1,690	7.04	10
11	Left in Business (Line 4 minus Line 10)		220	0.92	11
	EXTERNAL FINANCING:				
12	Increase in Creditors	+	90	0.38	12
13	Decrease in Debtors	+	—	—	13
14	Increase of Other Debts	+	—	—	14
15	Decrease of Other Credits	+	—	—	15
16	Total External Financing	=	90	0.38	16
17	CASH AT DISPOSAL (Line 11 plus Line 16)		310	1.30	17
	HOW THE MONEY WAS USED:				
18	Acquisitions	+	80	0.33	18
19	Increase in Debtors	+	110	0.46	19
20	Decrease in Creditors	+	—	—	20
21	Change in Inventory and WIP	+	30	0.12	21
22	Increase of Other Credits	+	10	0.04	22
23	Decrease of Other Debts	+	100	0.42	23
24	Total Capital Expenditures	=	330	1.38	24
25	CHANGE IN CASH (Line 17 minus Line 24)		− 20	−0.08	25

N.B. There are some unused lines (13, 14, 15 and 20). They are provided to cover the situation in which, for example debtors decrease instead of increase. A reduction in debtors indicates 'external financing' just as an increase in creditors would; that is to say, more money is received during the year than the total value of goods and services delivered.

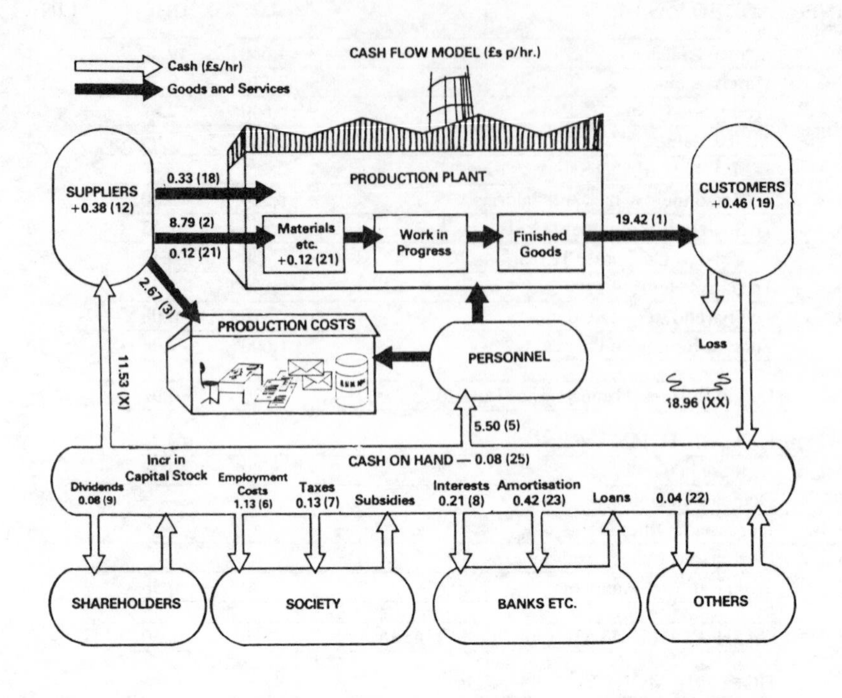

X) This is what we paid our suppliers:

	£s/hr
Acquisitions (18)	+ 0.33
Materials (2)	+ 8.79
INCR Inventory (21)	+ 0.12
Production Costs (3)	+ 2.67
INCR Creditors (12)	− 0.38
	11.53

XX) This is what our customers paid to us:

	£s/hr
Invoiced Sales (1)	+19.42
INCR Debtors (19)	0.46
	18.96

(Note: Figures within brackets refer to the line number on the INFRA table.)

A negative cash flow, such as the £20,000 in question is not necessarily alarming — particularly if it had been allowed for. Nevertheless, a firm cannot go on draining the cash indefinitely.

What could have been done to avoid this negative cash flow? If the employees had taken out £5.43 per hour in total instead of £5.50 the problem would have been solved and the employment cost of NHIC etc. would also have gone down by about 1p. The negative cash flow would also have been avoided if the owners (shareholders) had given up all their dividend. There are other alternatives. 12p per hour was used to increase inventory and work in progress. Was this necessary? Why did the customers get extra credit to the value of 46p per hour? The ability to pose these and similar questions is an essential part of the INFRA method.

Summary

So far we have considered:

- the added value
- the way in which the added value is distributed between interested parties
- what was left in the business.

We have also described:

- how much of the money used by the business came from outside
- the total funds available for use
- how this money was used
- what happened to the cash flowing in and out of the company.

Accountants refer to this kind of analysis as a 'Source and Application of Funds Statement'.

By showing this information in a diagram we can demonstrate the *cash flow* of Big Baker.

CASH FLOW (£000s)

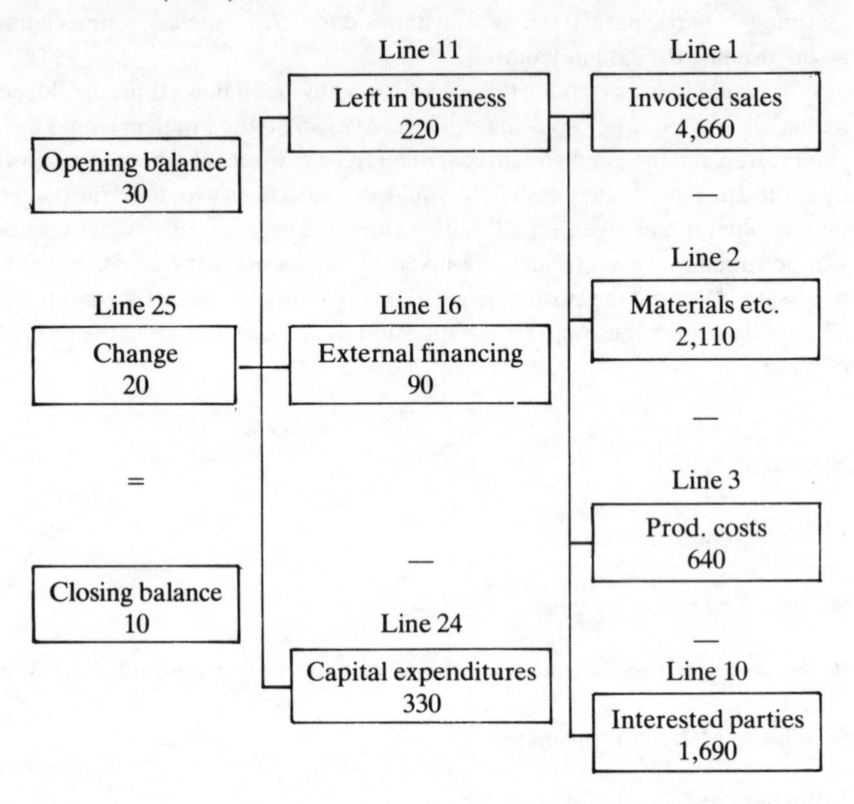

Before going further into Big Baker's accounts we must fully explain the concepts of Profit and Profitability. When we have done this it will be possible to understand the detail of the two main accounting documents — the profit and loss account and the balance sheet.

What is profit?

The concept of profit is one of our most frequently misunderstood notions — not least in political discussions when the listeners (and some of the speakers?) are often unaware of the real nature of the subject under consideration.

The first chapter dealt with 'money in and money out' and in the case of Big Baker Ltd. we came to the conclusion that cash in hand had been reduced by £20,000. Does this mean that there was a loss instead of a profit? Profit means that the assets of the company have increased: loss means that assets have decreased in real value allowing for changes in current price levels i.e. the effect of inflation. A change in the cash position does not tell the whole story of changes in assets — assets consist of more than cash.

What does it mean for a company to be 'richer'

A private individual can list his assets and liabilities on the 1st January each year and from it decide whether he has become richer or poorer in the course of the year, for example:—

	31.12.19X1	31.12.19X2
Assets	£	£
House	30,000	32,000
Car	4,500	3,800
Furniture etc.	6,000	6,500
Investments	3,000	3,300
Cash	700	400
	44,200	46,000
Liabilities		
Mortgage outstanding	12,000	11,000
Bank personal loan	800	1,100
	12,800	12,000
Net assets	31,400	34,000

During the year the household has become £2,600 richer. This statement is made with the proviso that the assets are correctly valued — no one can put an exact value on a house until it has been sold and paid for.

Fig. 5. A large fortune does not always mean more money in your pocket.

This example shows that a large fortune does not necessarily mean large amounts of easily available cash. We can become richer by increasing assets or reducing liabilities as we have done in the example — even though the cash in hand has fallen.

What profit did Big Baker make?

Business can take an annual 'snapshot' in just the same way as an individual. For a business also, profit is not the same as cash in hand: a business can also make a profit by increasing assets or reducing liabilities. What has actually happened to Big Baker?

Take the figures for assets from our table on page 29:

Line		£000s
18.	Fixed assets increased by	+ 80
19.	Debtors increased by	+110
21.	Inventory and W.I.P. (stocks) increased by	+ 30
22.	Short term investments increased by	+ 10
25.	Cash in hand reduced	– 20
	Net increase in assets	£210

In the same table the liabilities have changed by:

Line		£000s
12.	Creditors increased by	+ 90
23.	Bank loans reduced by	–100
	Dividends payable	– 20
	Net reduction in liabilities	– 30

A word of explanation is needed for dividends payable. The £20,000 paid in dividends to shareholders refers to the previous year. At the beginning of the present year the company owed £20,000 to the shareholders. This debt has been cancelled during the current year when the dividend was paid.

To summarise: assets have increased by £210,000 and liabilities decreased by £30,000. Total possessions (assets) of Big Baker have increased by £240,000.

Finally, there has been one other change in assets which has no effect on cash flow. The fixed assets (machinery, furniture etc.) have fallen in value over the year because of wear and tear — they have depreciated. An estimate has to be made to allow for the effect of this depreciation on the company's assets. Usually, a depreciation plan is set up. If it is estimated that a machine will last for five years; every year one-fifth of the purchase price is allowed in the accounts as depreciation so that after five years the machine has been fully depreciated and has an asset value of nil.

Big Baker has bought its equipment over a period of many years. Adding together all the amounts owed for depreciation in the present year we arrive at a figure of £60,000 — the allowance for depreciation in the current year.

To calculate the profit for the year, this figure for depreciation has to be taken from the previously calculated increase in asset values (£240,000) to give a total of £180,000 as Big Baker's profit for the year.

The profit and loss account

Our calculation has arrived at Big Baker's profit for the year by using the changes in assets and liabilities. Accountants use another method for calculating profit or loss. From the invoiced sales; all costs, except taxes, are deducted. The balance is referred to as 'Profits before tax'. Using this method Big Baker's profit would be expressed:

Where Does the Money Come From and Where Does It Go?

Line	Added Value	Total £000s	£s/hour
1.	Invoiced Sales	4,660	19.42
2.	Materials etc.	−2,110	− 8.79
3.	Production Costs	− 640	− 2.67
4.	Added Value	=1,910	= 7.96

Distribution to Participants

5.	To Personnel: wages and salaries	1,320	5.50
6.	To Society: Employment costs	270	1.13
7.	To Society: Taxes	30	0.13
8.	Bank Interest	50	0.21

What was the Result?

26.	Operating Profit (Line 4 minus line 5 minus line 6)	320	1.33
27.	Depreciation	60	0.25
28.	Profit after depreciation	260	1.08
29.	Profit before taxation (Line 28 minus line 8)	210	0.87

What is Profitability?

Profitability is a word used as frequently as profit and probably as much misunderstood. Our calculations show that Big Baker has made a profit of £210,000 before tax (line 29). Is that too big or too small? Is it excessive, enough or inadequate?

Profitability — a relative concept

Profit alone does not show whether a business performed well or not. To make it mean anything, profit must be compared with something.

If a friend says 'I received £500 in interest last year' he tells us very little. If he says 'last year I had £3,000 invested on which I received £500 in interest' we know rather more. His return was 16.67% which is more than he would have received by putting the money in a building society or bank deposit account. We can say that he had made a *profitable* investment.

On the other hand, he could have used the £3,000 as his capital to set up a small business; for instance, a hot dog stand. If, when he made up his accounts at the end of the year, he discovered that, after having paid all his expenses and given himself a reasonable salary, his capital had grown to £3,500 he will have earned £500 'interest' on his original capital. We refer to it as *return on capital* of 16.67%.

How to calculate profitability

Profitability is profit expressed as a percentage of the capital invested. The idea is very simple, but there are many problems and pitfalls in calculating profitability.

There are some general rules:

1. The profit figure used for the calculation is *profit after depreciation but before paying loan interest*. The reason for calculating profitability is to show what return (interest) the use of the capital yields. Whether he used his own money or borrowed from someone else our hot dog dealer's profitability is 16.67%.

2. Assets are reduced by the total of creditors. This is because suppliers do not usually charge for supplying and do not ask for a return on the capital employed in supplying you with goods for which payment has not been made.

Having made these adjustments, the capital figure used for profitability calculations is referred to as 'capital employed'.

To calculate the profitability of Big Baker we first need the profit figure from line 28.

		£000s	£s/hr
26.	Operating Profit before Depreciation (Line 4 minus line 5 minus line 6)	320	1.33
27.	Depreciation	− 60	−0.25
28.	Profit after Depreciation	=260	=1.08

Then calculate capital employed, as at 1st January

	£000s
Cash in hand	+ 30
Debtors	+ 510
Other credits	+ 30
Inventory, W.I.P.	+ 120
Creditors	− 310
Net current assets	= 380
Fixed assets	+ 720
Capital employed	=1,100

The return on capital employed (ROC) is $\frac{260 \times 100}{1{,}100} = 23.6\%$.

N.B. To simplify the calculation, the calculations have been based on the state of the company on 1st January. It is more accurate to use an average of the opening and closing capital position. This would have given ROC of 23.0% instead of 23.6%.

An even better idea of profitability is given by the calculation of two subordinate ratios.

(a) *Profit margin* is profit as a percentage of sales.

(b) *Turn over rate* is the number of times in a year that capital employed is 'turned around'. It is calculated by dividing sales by capital employed.

All of these ratios and figures can be combined in one diagram, which we will refer to as a 'Profitability Tree'.

PROFITABILITY TREE

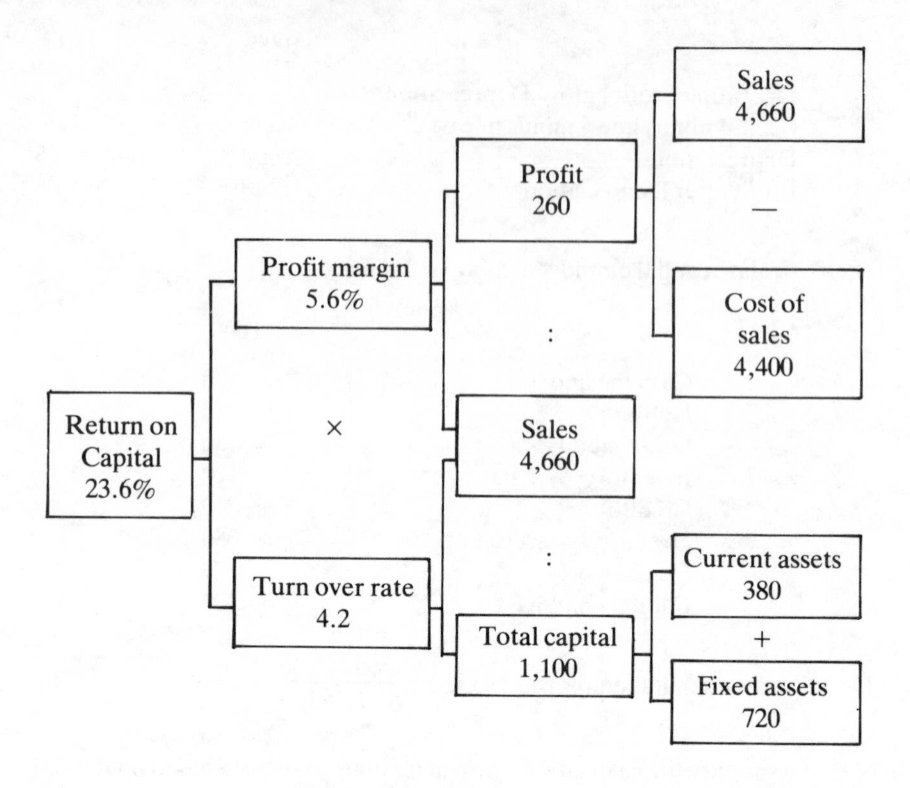

The figures and the diagram tell us that:

- Big Baker is very profitable.
- In present conditions it is more advantageous for the owners of Big Baker to have their money invested in the business, than in the bank.

In making these broad statements we must remember that:

- Running a business is more risky than investing money in the bank.
- Good years will be followed by bad years. During the good years reserves will have to be built up for bad years.

- Out of the profit before tax, the shareholders only took £20,000 in dividends. If we assume that they pay 30% tax, they only have £14,000 to spend. This is the only share of the profit used for private consumption. All the rest was used to buy assets, amortise loans or pay tax.

- Cash in hand was reduced by £20,000. This could indicate that the profit was not enough.

How can these figures be used?

There are many pitfalls in calculating profitability. Like statistics, profitability calculations can be used to prove almost anything. By making the following legitimate assumptions, the profitability of Big Baker can easily be reduced.

- Because the machines have been working continuously days and nights, we could double the depreciation allowance from £60,000 to £120,000 on the grounds that they have done two years' work in one. Profit is thus reduced by £60,000.

- A careful examination of the year end stock could identify part of the goods as unsaleable, possibly reducing this value from £120,000 to £90,000. The £30,000 is an expense to be deducted from profit and the total of capital employed reduced by the same amount.

- Fixed assets could be revalued to allow for increases in the cost of new machines of the same kind. Let us assume that by this means we increase the value of fixed assets from £720,000 to £1,000,000: an increase of £280,000 in capital employed.

These adjustments would have the following effects on profitability:

- Profit is reduced by £90,000 (£60,000 plus £30,000).

- Capital employed is increased by £250,000 (£280,000 — £30,000) to give the following changes in the profitability ratio:

BEFORE

$$\frac{260 \times 100}{1{,}100} = 23.6\%$$

AFTER

$$\frac{170 \times 100}{1{,}350} = 12.6\%$$

These amendments are based on judgment and do not affect the real position. Nevertheless they show how difficult it is to be precise when talking of profitability.

Fig. 6. Profitability is a very elastic concept.

Evaluation of assets

The value placed on the assets of the business is a major factor in calculating profitability. Unless we observe certain rules, we can produce any figure for profitability that we want.

Fortunately, there are such rules, which can be summarised briefly as:

- The *civil law* puts an *upper* limit on asset valuation. Without some such control a business on the verge of insolvency could be made to look prosperous by inflating the value of the assets; to the prejudice of bankers, suppliers and other people doing business with the company. The value of stocks must be vouched for by independent auditors.
- Regulations covering *returns for taxation* purposes do not allow unlimited depreciation as an expense for tax purposes thereby putting a *lower* limit on asset valuation. As taxation is based on profit; by under-valuing assets, companies could reduce annual profit and thus reduce liability for tax.

The limitations are not restrictive in an operational sense and do not hamper companies in the way in which they are run. By using the full extent of the regulations it is possible for companies to plan their tax load: but this is not a topic for the present book.

How to interpret the two critical business documents

We can now study the profit and loss account and the balance sheet. There are certain rules which decide what information should appear in these documents and how it must be presented. Every year these documents have to be completed and returns made to the Inland Revenue and to Companies House. The accounts prepared for the Inland Revenue are used for the purpose of calculating tax liability. The Registrar of Companies requires a completely separate set of accounts which show the asset value and the profitability of the company. These latter accounts are available for anyone to view on the payment of a small fee.

This chapter began by showing Big Baker's profit and loss account and balance sheet. In the course of the chapter these figures have nearly all been analysed using tables and diagrams.

On the following pages, the early part of the model and the table give the full details of all the figures to which we have referred. In the model, as well as in the profit & loss account and balance sheet of this chapter, the figures in brackets indicate the line numbers on the table and show where the INFRA approach puts each of these sums of money in its description of the working of the firm.

The Profit and Loss Account (See page 22)

Line 29 on the table (Profit before tax) is the real measure of the success of the business. It is calculated by deducting all costs (except taxes) from invoiced sales. The figure remaining is £210,000.

Net profit (line 31) is what remains when tax is taken from profit before tax. In this case, net profit is £180,000.

X) This is what we paid our suppliers:

Acquisitions (18)	+ 80
Material (2)	+2,110
INCR Inventory (21)	+ 30
Production Cost (3)	+ 640
INCR Creditors (12)	− 90
	=2,770

XX) This is what our customers paid us:

Invoiced Sales (1)	+4,660
INCR Debtors (19)	− 110
	=4,550

(Note: Figures within brackets refer to the line number on the INFRA table.)

CASH FLOW MODEL (£'000s)

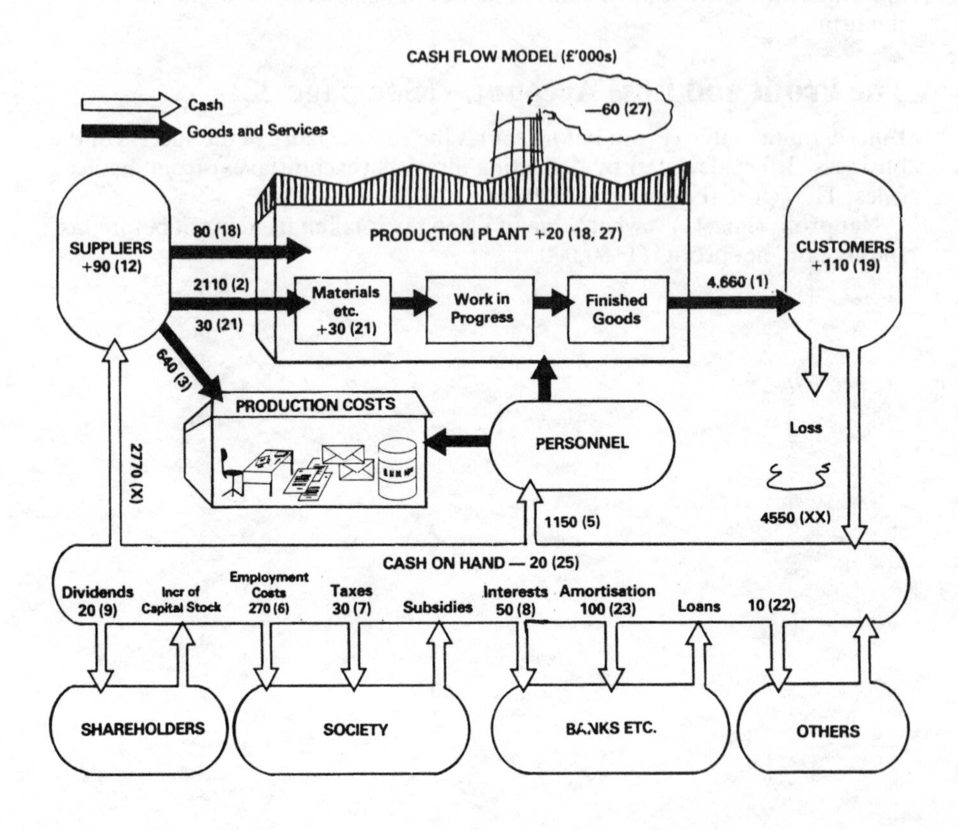

Where Does the Money Come From and Where Does It Go?

LINE	ADDED VALUE		£000	£/Hr	LINE
1	Invoiced Sales	+	4,660	19.42	1
2	Materials etc.	−	2,110	8.79	2
3	Production Costs	−	640	2.67	3
4	Added Value	=	1,910	7.96	4
	TO PARTICIPANTS:				
5	To Personnel: Wages and Salaries	+	1,320	5.50	5
6	To Society: Employment Costs	+	270	1.13	6
7	Corporate Taxes	+	30	0.13	7
8	To Banks etc: Interests	+	50	0.21	8
9	To Shareholders: Dividends	+	20	0.08	9
10	Total to Interested Parties	=	1,690	7.04	10
11	Left in Business (Line 4 minus Line 10)		220	0.92	11
	EXTERNAL FINANCING:				
12	Increase in Creditors	+	90	0.38	12
13	Decrease in Debtors	+	—	—	13
14	Increase of Other Debts	+	—	—	14
15	Decrease of Other Credits	+	—	—	15
16	Total External Financing	=	90	0.38	16
17	CASH AT DISPOSAL (Line 11 plus Line 16)		310	1.30	17
	HOW THE MONEY WAS USED:				
18	Acquisitions	+	80	0.33	18
19	Increase in Debtors	+	110	0.46	19
20	Decrease in Creditors	+	—	—	20
21	Change in Inventory and WIP	+	30	0.12	21
22	Increase of Other Credits	+	10	0.04	22
23	Decrease of Other Debts	+	100	0.42	23
24	Total Capital Expenditures	=	330	1.38	24
25	CHANGE IN CASH (Line 17 minus Line 24)		− 20	−0.08	25
	WHAT WAS THE RESULT?				
26	Operating Profit Before Depreciations (Line 4 minus Line 5 minus Line 6)		320	1.33	26
27	Depreciations	−	60	0.25	27
28	Profit after Depreciations	=	260	1.08	28
29	Profit Before Taxes (Line 28 minus Line 8)		210	0.87	29
30	Corporate Taxes (= Line 7)	−	30	0.13	30
31	Net Profit (Line 29 minus Line 30)	=	180	0.75	31

The Balance Sheet (See page 23)

The balance sheet has two sections — *assets* and *liabilities* (including equity and reserves) — and is a snapshot, taken at the end of the financial year. The flow of goods and services is 'frozen' momentarily: all the values are counted and the results presented in a picture composed of financial values.

Balance sheets are drawn up to examine two features — the standing of the company at the end of the year and the extent to which this standing has changed compared with twelve months previously. The standard way of laying out a balance sheet is to show figures for both this year and last. For ease of comparison the balance sheet on page 23 shows what changes there have been as a third column.

Fig. 7. The balance sheet is like an X-ray: a snapshot that may show that something is amiss.

A few notes in explanation of the figures are needed.

Current assets are assets that flow continuously through the business, for example — cash, stocks, debtors etc.

Fixed assets are, on the contrary, things that are meant to be kept — land, buildings, machinery, furniture. The balance sheet shows the accumulated value of Big Baker's assets to be £1,240,000 — an increase over the previous year of £80,000 — this year's acquisitions. The accumulated depreciation figure is £500,000 — £60,000 has been added this year to last year's accumulated figure of £440,000. The current *net value* of fixed assets is £740,000 (£1,240,000 purchase value less £500,000 of accumulated depreciation). These values are intelligent and reasonable estimates. The only way to find the actual value of the business is to try to sell it and see what a potential buyer is prepared to offer.

Current liabilities are liabilities that have to be cleared within the next twelve months. The remaining liabilities are classed as *long term liabilities*.

Equity consists of the initial capital put in by the founders of the company plus any further increments of capital and profits retained in the business.

TWO IMPORTANT RATIOS

Equity Ratio and Quick Ratio

In addition to giving the value of the assets (cash, debtors, goods, machinery etc.) the balance sheet shows where the money has come from to run the business: from banks, suppliers, taxation due but not yet paid etc. What is left of the assets when all liabilities have been deducted is the shareholders' share of the business: the equity. In our example the equity is £280,000. The *equity ratio* is the equity as a percentage of the Total Assets. This is approximately 17.9% of the total assets of £1,560,000: in the previous year it was 8.5%. Put the other way round it means that 82.1% of the company's assets are 'owned' by outsiders — banks, suppliers, Inland Revenue etc. A low *equity ratio* means that the firm has limited freedom to do what it wants. Sometimes for a company with a poor *equity ratio* a major source of funds (e.g. a bank) may claim seats on the Board of Directors and thus exercise some direct control.

The only ways in which a company can improve its *equity ratio* are by:

1. Persuading the shareholders to put more money into the firm.

2. Retaining profits in the business instead of distributing them to the shareholders in dividends.

A sound *equity ratio* is essential if jobs are to be secure. Only profitable businesses can improve it: nobody is willing to invest in a loss-making company.

Whether or not the *equity ratio* is considered satisfactory will depend upon the type of business and the size and structure of the company but most authorities usually look for about 30%.

The *quick ratio* expresses the ease with which assets can be turned into cash. Such assets are cash, bank accounts, debtors and other short term credits — a matter of £670,000 (£10,000 cash, £620,000 debtors, £40,000 short-term investments) in the case of Big Baker. The short-term liabilities (creditors £400,000, other current liabilities £240,000) total £640,000. The *quick ratio* is therefore $\frac{6.7}{6.4} = 1.05$. A good *quick ratio* (anything over 1.0) indicates better chances of survival and the ability to cope with sudden changes in cash flow.

Who gained most from Big Baker's activities?

Profit is a very controversial word — often qualified by the words 'excessive' or 'indecent'. Such words infer that the shareholders have been given an unreasonable share of the income at the expense of other interested parties. The answer to the question 'who gained most?' can be seen by examining the final distribution of the added value.

Personnel: Wages and salaries totalled £1,320,000. Out of this the recipients have to pay personal taxes. If we assume that average personal taxation is 22%; the employees keep 78% or about £1,030,000.

Society: Society receives personal taxes from the employees, corporate and individual contributions to the costs of employment, local taxes and corporate taxes. Shareholders also pay tax on dividends — presently 30%. In the £20,000 of dividends this tax will amount to £6,000. In addition, of course, Society will profit from indirect taxes (VAT, drinks tax, petrol tax etc.) from the money spent by shareholders and employees. It is not possible to take this into account because of variations in individual expenditure and we must express society's share of Big Baker's years work as

	£s
Employees' income tax	290,000
Employment costs	270,000
Corporate taxes	30,000
Tax on dividends	6,000
	596,000

Banks etc: £60,000 has been paid to the banks in interest. At the same time Big Baker has received interest on their money in the bank. The result is a net payment to the bank of £50,000.

Shareholders: £20,000 was paid out in dividends on which £6,000 was paid in tax; leaving £14,000 for the shareholders.

The final distribution

	£000s	£s/h
To personnel	1,030	4.29
To society	596	2.48
To banks	50	0.21
To shareholders	14	0.06
Left in business	220	0.92
Total value added	1,910	7.96

We can see that if Big Baker performs well, has a high figure for added value and makes a profit, Society will be one of the main beneficiaries.

Fig. 8. When a business is performing well and increases its added value, Society gets one of the biggest pieces of the cake.

The opposite is also true. If Big Baker makes a loss, tax payments reduce and, if Big Baker goes out of business and cannot provide jobs, Society gets less money in taxes. In addition, Society has to cope with all of the problems arising from the unemployed.

Big Baker's distribution of added value is typical of business in general.

Job security

Big Baker's business has been examined from several points of view, but one question remains unanswered — how safe are the jobs?

There is, unfortunately, no positive answer to this question. A consultant's analysis is much like a medical diagnosis. The doctor carries out a number of tests and analyses them: he questions the patient and takes X rays — all as part of the input for his diagnosis. After diagnosing, he recommends treatment or says that all is well and nothing needs to be done. The doctor will not, however, discover a small cancer that does not hurt yet: nor can he guarantee that the patient will not get influenza or be hurt in an accident.

We have made the following 'medical tests' on Big Baker:

Cash flow analysis: Cash in hand has been reduced by £20,000. This is not necessarily serious but cash flow has to be watched carefully.

Profitability analysis: Return on capital is 23.6% which is very good.

Analysis of Equity Ratio: The present E.R. is 17.9%. In the previous year it was only 8.5%. An acceptable figure would be 30%. The trend is satisfactory but must be continued.

Analysis of quick ratio: This ratio is 1.05, which is satisfactory.

A doctor would consider the patient in good health. A healthy firm means safe jobs. Big Baker typifies a prosperous, expanding company.

3 · Computerisation of the INFRA method

Chapter 2 was full of figures and calculations. To relieve the businessman of this task of calculation and to allow him to concentrate on the creative tasks of business analysis and budgeting, the INFRA method is also available as a computer program. This program has, among others, versions for the IBM and Hewlett-Packard Personal Computers. Chapter 3 describes the program and its possibilities by analysing the annual report of a British company — Darlington & Simpson Rolling Mills plc — for 1985.

DSRM

Darlington & Simpson Rolling Mills plc completed fifty years in business in 1985. The company, a world leader in the hot rolling of special profiles in steel, was founded on 7th June, 1935 by the amalgamation of Darlington Rolling Mills, F. R. Simpson of Oldbury, Birmingham and J. & W. Marshall of Walsall. By 1937 the whole production plant was on the Rise Carr site at Darlington where steel rolling had been started in 1865 by Fry I'anson & Co.

By sound management, a far-sighted investment policy and the maintenance of high quality products, the company has prospered and expanded over the years; specialising in high quality, high technology products. Concentration on exports has been such that in 1985 out of a turnover of £38,791,000 no less than £30,316,000 (78.2%) went for export. The company was among the first recipients of the Queen's Award to Industry in 1966 and has been honoured in this way subsequently in 1970, 1972, 1977 and 1983. In 1969 The International Export Association elected DSRM as its 'Company of the Year'. In the past decade, which has seen severe depression in the steel industry, DSRM has never failed to return a profit — the worst year being 1983 with a return on sales of 3.5%.

DSRM has been using the concept of added value in analysing financial results for several years and was an obvious company for Infra to approach when a U.K. example was needed for this book.

The writers' thanks are due to Mr. Derrick Hale (Financial Director) for making the 1985 figures available and, in its Jubilee year, we wish the company every success in the future.

The Annual Report

The Annual Report, which includes the Profit and Loss Account, The Balance Sheet and the Sources and Application of Funds, is the basis of this analysis of DSRM results. The figures marked (*) on these documents are those used to compile the Infra analysis.

DARLINGTON & SIMPSON
ROLLING MILLS Plc

Group Profit & Loss Account

For the year ended 30th March 1985

	Notes	**1985 £000**	1984 £000
Turnover	2	* **38,791**	27,676
Cost of sales	3	**(28,641)**	(23,229)
Gross profit		**10,150**	4,447
Distribution costs		**(4,736)**	(2,708)
Operating profit		**5,414**	1,739
Interest receivable		* **123**	72
Profit before interest payable		**5,537**	1,811
Interest payable	4	*(**195)**	
Profit on ordinary activities before taxation	5	**5,342**	
Taxation on profit on ordinary activities	7	*(**2,545)**	(659)
Profit on ordinary activities after taxation		**2,797**	977
Extraordinary item	8	—	1,032
Profit for the financial year	9	**2,797**	2,009
Dividends	10	*(**1,678)**	(586)
Profit retained	19	**1,119**	1,423

DARLINGTON & SIMPSON
ROLLING MILLS Plc

Group Balance Sheets

At 30th March 1985

	Notes	1985	1984
Fixed assets			
Tangible assets	11	***10,987**	10,207
Investments	12	—	—
		10,987	10,207
Currents assets			
Stocks	13	*** 5,059**	3,306
Debtors	14	**6,932**	5,583
Cash at Bank and in hand		*** 1,840**	1,663
		13,831	10,552
Current liabilities			
Creditors: amounts falling due within one year	15	**(8,962)**	(8,304)
Net current assets		**4,869**	2,248
Total assets less current liabilities		**15,856**	12,455
Creditors: amounts falling due after more than one year	16	**(3,493)**	(1,346)
Provision for liabilities and charges	17	**(1,971)**	(2,021)
		10,392	9,088
Capital and reserves			
Called up share capital	18	**5,000**	5,000
Revaluation reserve	19	**771**	596
Other reserves	19	**10**	—
Profit and loss account	19	**4,611**	3,492
		***10,392**	9,088

J T Carter
D B Hale Directors

Accounts approved by the Board of Directors on 16th May 1985

DARLINGTON & SIMPSON
ROLLING MILLS Plc

Notes on the accounts

	1985 £000	1984 £000
5 PROFIT ON ORDINARY ACTIVITIES BEFORE TAXATION		
An analysis of group profit on ordinary activities before taxation by activity is given below		
Hot rolled steel profiles	**5,339**	1,636
Steel fabrication and engineering contracting	**3**	—
	5,342	1,636
Profit on ordinary activities before taxation is stated after charging		
Depreciation (Note 11)	* **1,180**	994
Loss on disposal of fixed assets	**46**	74
Hire of plant and machinery	**80**	61
Auditors remuneration	**22**	19
Foreign currency translation loss/(gain) on consolidation	**51**	(11)
Directors emoluments (Note 6)		
As directors	**11**	11
As executives	**174**	160

6 EMPLOYEES

Average number of persons, including directors, employed by the group during the year

	1985	1984
Works	**524**	524
Staff	**121**	117
	* **645**	641

	1985 £000	1984 £000
Employment costs for the above persons		
Wages and salaries	* **5,400**	4,441
Social security costs	* **524**	478
Other pension costs	**345**	308
	6,269	5,227
Directors emoluments excluding pension contributions		
Chairman	**2**	2
Highest paid director	**48**	44

Other directors	1985	1984
£0-£ 5,000	**7**	5
£30,001-£35,000	**2**	3
£35,001-£40,000	**1**	—

DARLINGTON & SIMPSON
ROLLING MILLS Plc

Notes on the accounts

Continued

		GROUP	
		1985	1984
		£000	£000
14	**DEBTORS**		
	Amounts falling due within one year		
	Trade debtors	* **6,324**	5,291
	Amounts owed by subsidiaries	**—**	—
	Other debtors	* **574**	258
	Prepayments and accrued income	**34**	34
		6,932	5,583
	Included above are amounts due after more than one year	**—**	
15	**CREDITORS**		
	Amounts falling due within one year		
	Current instalments on medium term loan	* **—**	218
	Bank overdraft	**83**	—
	Trade creditors	* **5,644**	6,548
	Proposed final dividend	**1,192**	51
	Corporation tax	**409**	73
	Other taxation and social security	**245**	169
	Other creditors	**45**	79
	Accruals and deferred income	**1,344**	706
	Amounts owed to subsidiaries	**—**	—
		8,962	8,304
16	**CREDITORS**		
	Amounts fallIng due after more than one year		
	Medium term loans wholly repayable within five years		
	Midland Bank Plc	**—**	218
	European Coal and Steel Community	**800**	800
		800	1,018
	Less current instalments (Note 15)	**—**	(218)
		* **800**	800
	Corporation tax due 1st July 1986	**2,569**	406
	Government grants	**124**	140
		3,493	1,346

The loan from the European Coal and Steel Community is in sterling and is repayable in one instalment on 7th March 1988.

For non-accountants it is difficult to grasp the full meaning of an official annual report. To present a more easy to read version, it is necessary to select essential figures and put them into the Infra table from which they can be analysed.

The first set of key information is that from which added value is calculated:

What is the value of sales?
What is the cost of the materials used?
What were the production costs?

To know how the added value has been distributed we need to know:

The total of wages and salaries
Employment costs
Local and corporate taxes
Interest paid
Dividends paid to shareholders

To calculate 'the amount of External Financing utilised' and to say 'how the money was used' we need to know *assets* and *liabilities* of the company on the first and last days of the financial year.

Assets

Cash in hand
Debtors
Inventory, work in progress
Other credits
Fixed assets at acquisition value
less depreciation
equals book value of Fixed Assets

Liabilities

Creditors
Overdrawings on current account
Bank loans
Other debts

These key figures are marked with an * on the Profit and Loss Account and Balance Sheet information on the preceding pages. Some of the figures which are needed are not usually quoted in the annual report. They appear as part of 'Operating Costs' in the Profit and Loss Account and have to be extracted from the company's internal records. They include:

Cost of materials used
Production costs
Wages and salaries
Employment costs
Hours worked — figures of hours worked can be calculated by multiplying the number of employees by the average numbers of hours worked per employee each year.

Data Input

The key figures have then to be entered on the special Infra Data Input Sheet. The accompanying tables show the completed Data Input Sheet for DSRM for 1985.

INFRA method INPUT DATA	Date: 19.2.86 Sign.:

Company: D.S.R.M.   Period: 1985

VAT-factor: ______

(x) Actual
( ) Budget
( ) Forecast

Employees 645 x hours/year 2048 = hours worked ________°

Investment income 123

PROFIT & LOSS ITEMS

Line		Total £000	
1	Invoiced sales ....+	38791	·
2	Materials etc ....−	19396	·
3	Production costs .....−	6532	·
4	Value added ....=		°
5	Wages & salaries .....+	5400	
6	Employment costs .....+	869	
7	Corporate taxes ......+	2545	
8	Interests net ....+	72	
9	Dividends ....+	1678	
10	To interested parties =		°
11	Left in business		°

° Computed automatically

· Computed automatically if product groups are used

Others must be given

BALANCE ITEMS:

Line			Opening balance			Closing balance
1	Cash in hand ....+		1663		+	°
2	Debtors ....+		5291		+	6324
3	Inventory, WIP ....+		2306		+	5059
4	Other credits ....+		292		+	608
5	Fixed assets ...+	10207		+	12167	
6	Depreciations ..−			−	1180	
7	F.A. book value =		°	=		°
8	Total assets ....=		°		=	°
9	Creditors ....+		6548		+	5644
10	Current account ....+		218		+	83
11	Bank loans etc ....+		800		+	800
12	Borrowing need (0 init'lly)+		xxxxxxxxxxx		+	°
13	Other debts ....+		4105		+	8084
14	Total liabilities ....+		°		+	°
15	Shareholders' equity		°		=	°

Inventory adjustment _______ (Only in certain cases. See manual)

This information can then be fed to the computer. The computer carries out the necessary calculations and presents an analysis on a video screen or as a print out.

The complete analysis

The complete Infra analysis of information for DSRM for 1985 follows:

INFRA method
DSRM Actual 1985

	LINE	£000	£/Hr.	
Invoiced Sales	1	38791	29.37	
Materials etc	2	19396	14.68	Added Value
Production Costs	3	6532	4.94	
Added Value	**4**	**12863**	**9.74**	
Wages & Salaries	5	5400	4.09	
Employment Costs	6	869	0.66	
Corporate Taxes	7	2345	1.93	
Interests	8	72	0.05	Distribution of Added Value
Dividends	9	1678	1.27	
To Interested Parties	10	10564	8.00	
Left in Business	**11**	**2299**	**1.74**	
Incr Creditors	12	0	0.00	
Decr Debtors	13	0	0.00	
Incr Other Debts	14	3844	2.91	
Decr Other Crs	15	0	0.00	
Ext Financing	16	3844	2.91	
Cash at Disposal	**17**	**6143**	**4.65**	
Acquisitions	18	1960	1.48	Funds Statement
Incr Debtors	19	1033	0.78	
Decr Creditors	20	904	0.68	
Change Inventory	21	1753	1.33	
Incr Other Crs	22	316	0.24	
Decr Other Debts	23	0	0.00	
Tot Expenditurs	**24**	**5966**	**4.52**	
Change in Cash	**25**	**177**	**0.13**	
Profit Bef Depr	26	6594	4.99	
Depreciations	27	1180	0.89	
Profit Aft Depr	28	5414	4.10	
Profit Bef Tax	**29**	**5342**	**4.04**	Profit & Loss Account
Corporate Taxes	30	2545	1.93	
Net Profit	32	2797	2.12	

Capital Employed	33	11090	
Turnover Rate	34	3.50	
Profit Margin	25	14.27	
Return on Capit	**36**	**49.93**	Ratios
Equity	37	10207	
Return on Equity	38	52.34	
Equity Ratio	39	41.13	

	LINE	OPENING	CLOSING	
Cash in Hand	1	1663	1840	
Debtors	2	5291	6324	
Inventory, WIP	3	3306	5059	
Other Credits	4	292	608	
Fixed Assets	5	10207	12167	
Depreciations	6	0	1180	
F.A. Book Value	7	10207	10987	
Total Assets	**8**	**20759**	**24818**	Balance Sheet
Creditors	9	6548	5644	
Current Account	10	218	83	
Bank Loans etc	11	800	800	
Borrowing Need	12	0	0	
Other Debts	13	4105	8084	
Tot Liab'ties	**14**	**11671**	**14611**	
Equity	15	9088	10207	

— INFRA UK —

These figures tell us that 1985 was a very successful year. Added value per hour of £9.74 covers the claims from interested parties of £8.00 per hour, leaving £1.74 per hour in the business. Is that enough? Ideally, it should cover the year's acquisitions and allow for a bit to be put on one side for the future. The Funds Statement shows the major expenditures as:

Acquisitions	£1.48 per hour
Increase in debtors	£0.78 per hour
Increase in inventory	£1.33 per hour
Total	£3.59 per hour

This amount is much more than the amount 'left in the business' and indicates that £1.74 is certainly not too much.

Profitability (£000s)

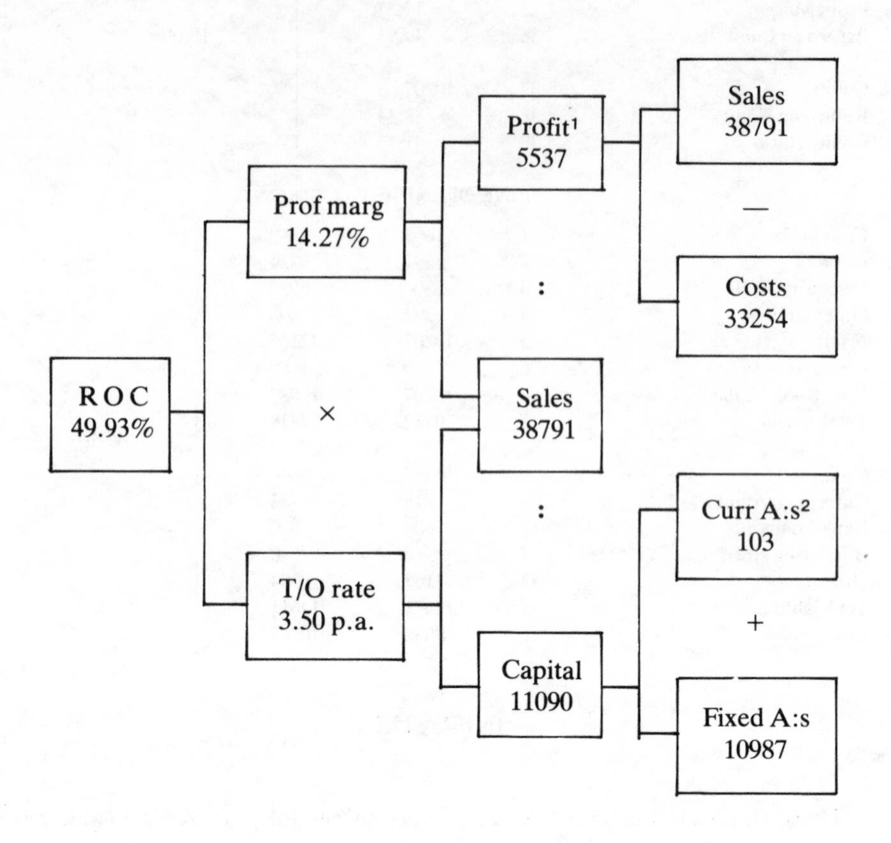

[1] Line 28 + interest from Group profit and loss account.

[2] Closing balance items 1, 2, 3 and 4 less items 9 and 13.

The business yields a very satisfactory return on capital employed (ROC) of 49.93%. But even a good result can be improved upon. If operating costs and capital employed could have been reduced by 3%, the ROC would have been almost 61%!

Cash Flow (£000s)

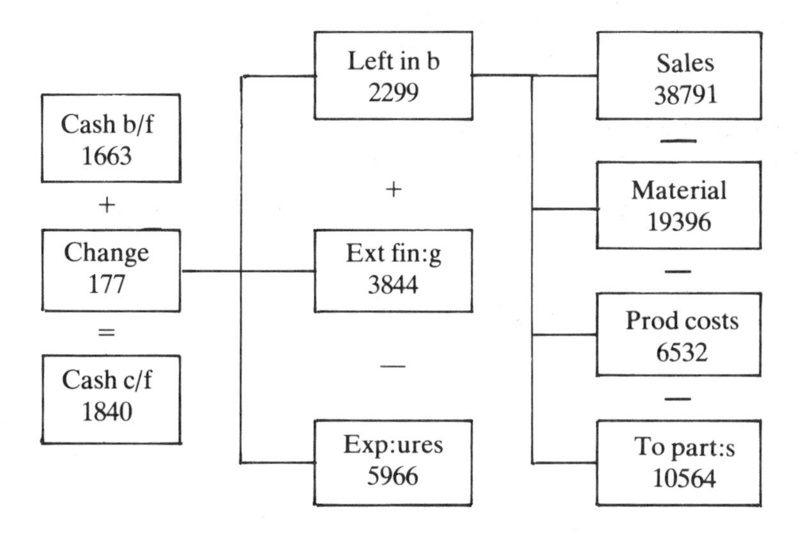

Borrowing need: 0

The increase in cash in hand is £177,000 or £0.13 per hour. Consider, however, the increase in other debts! Without this as a source of finance there would actually be a negative cash flow of £3,667,000 — about £2.78 per hour. This illustrates again that the future of a business depends not only on productivity but also on being able to manage cash flow and on having access to bank and other funds.

What would happen if . . .

The computer can be used to change certain features of the business scene and immediately to show the results of these changes. What would have happened if, for example, DSRM had:

raised prices by 1%
reduced material usage by 1%
saved 1% on production costs

without changing any other factors?

The answer is shown in the second Profitability Tree.

Prices up 1% — Materials down 1% — Production costs down 1%

PROFITABILITY TREE

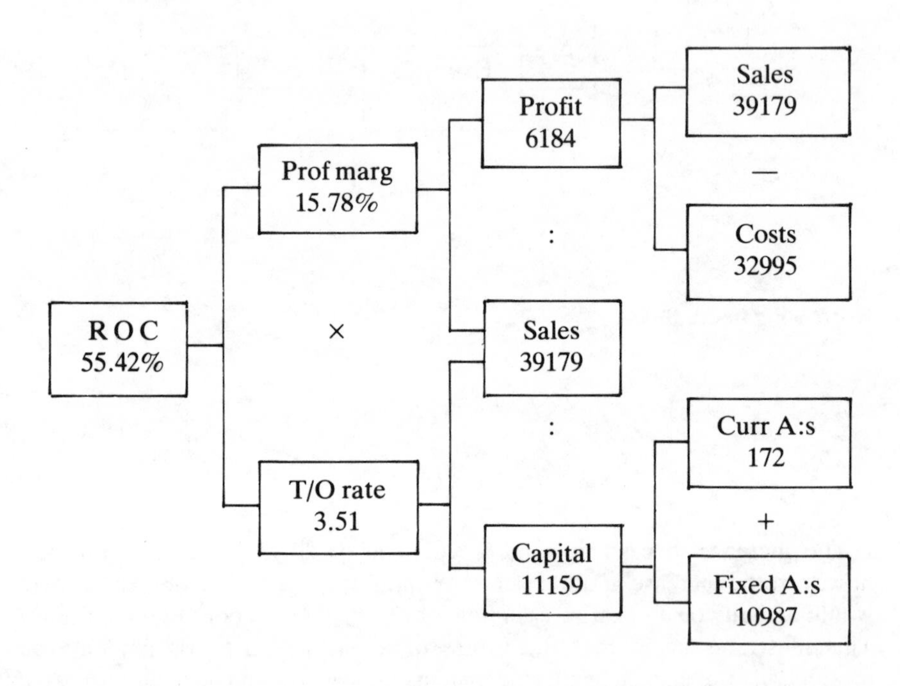

Drawing up a budget

One of the uses to which the figures for the annual results can be put is that of budgeting for the following financial year; to help with future decision making. In drawing up a budget for DSRM for 1986, the starting point is the actual outcome of the 1985 trading. Assume that discussions with the top management team (sales, production, personnel, accounts) have produced the following practical preliminary assumptions for 1986.

- Volume will be the same as 1985 but prices will be up by 5%.
- Material prices and production costs will be up by 10%.
- The same numbers of personnel will be employed as 1985 but wages will be up by 8%.
- Investment income will be £120,000: interest to be paid will be £250,000.
- Taxation, dividends, acquisitions and depreciation will be as for 1985.
- Debtors, inventory and creditors to be adjusted to the new assumed price levels.

For these anticipated changes a new Data Input Sheet can be prepared and fed into the computer. The Data Input Sheet and the computer printout are on the following pages.

INFRA method INPUT DATA	Date: 22.2.86 Sign.:

Company: DSRM Period: 1986

VAT-factor:

[ ] Actual
[X] Budget
[ ] Forecast

Employees 645 x hours/year 2048 = hours worked ____ °

Investment income 120

PROFIT & LOSS ITEMS

Line		Total £000	
1	Invoiced sales ....+	40730	·
2	Materials etc ....−	21335	·
3	Production costs ......−	7185	
4	Value added ....−		°
5	Wages & salaries ......+	5830	
6	Employment costs ......+	940	
7	Corporate taxes ....+	2545	
8	Interests net ....+	130	
9	Dividends ....+	1680	
10	To interested parties =		°
11	Left in business		°

° Computed automatically

· Computed automatically if product groups are used

Others must be given

BALANCE ITEMS:

Line			Opening balance			Closing balance
1	Cash in hand ....+		1840		+	°
2	Debtors ....+		6324		+	6640
3	Inventory, WIP ....+		5059		+	5565
4	Other credits ....+		608		+	608
5	Fixed assets ...+	12167		14127	+	
6	Depreciations ..−	1180		2360		
7	F.A. book value =		°		=	°
8	Total assets ....=		°		=	°
9	Creditors ....+		5644		+	6210
10	Current account ....+		83		+	83
11	Bank loans etc ....+		800		+	800
12	Borrowing need (0 init'lly)+		xxxxxxxxxxx		+	°
13	Other debts ....+		8084		+	8084
14	Total liabilities ....+		°		+	°
15	Shareholders' equity		°		=	°

Inventory adjustment (Only in certain cases. See manual)

INFRA method
DSRM Budget 1986

	LINE	£000	£/H	
Invoiced Sales	1	40730	30.83	Added Value
Materials etc	2	21335	16.15	
Production Costs	3	7185	5.44	
Added Value	**4**	**12210**	**9.24**	
Wages & Salaries	5	5830	4.41	Distribution of Added Value
Employment Costs	6	940	0.71	
Corporate Taxes	7	2545	1.93	
Interest	8	130	0.10	
Dividends	9	1680	1.27	
To Int Parties	10	11125	8.42	
Left in Business	**11**	**1085**	**0.82**	
Incr Creditors	12	566	0.43	Funds Statement
Decr Debtors	13	0	0.00	
Incr Other Debts	14	0	0.00	
Decr Other Crs	15	0	0.00	
Ext Financing	16	566	0.43	
Cash at Disposal	**17**	**1651**	**1.25**	
Acquisitions	18	1960	1.48	
Incr Debtors	19	316	0.24	
Decr Creditors	20	0	0.00	
Change Inventory	21	506	0.38	
Incr Other Crs	22	0	0.00	
Decr Other Debts	23	0	0.00	
Tot Expenditures	**24**	**2782**	**2.11**	
Change in Cash	25	−1131	−0.86	
Profit Bef Depr	26	5440	4.12	Profit & Loss Account
Depreciations	27	1180	0.89	
Profit Aft Depr	28	4260	3.22	
Profit Bef Tax	**29**	**4130**	**3.13**	
Corporate Taxes	30	2545	1.93	
Net Profit	32	1585	1.20	
Capital Employed	33	10995		Ratios
Turnover Rate	34	3.70		
Profit Margin	35	10.75		
Return on Capit	**36**	**39.84**		
Equity	37	10112		
Return on Equity	38	40.84		
Equity Ratio	**39**	**39.99**		

	LINE	OPENING	CLOSING	
Cash in Hand	1	1840	709	Balance Sheet
Debtors	2	6324	6640	
Inventory, WIP	3	5059	5565	
Other Credits	4	608	608	
Fixed Assets	5	12167	14127	
Depreciations	6	1180	2360	
F.A. Book Value	7	10987	11767	
Total Assets	**8**	**24818**	**25289**	
Creditors	9	5644	6210	
Current Account	10	83	83	
Bank Loans etc	11	800	800	
Borrowing Need	12	0	0	
Other Debts	13	8084	8084	
Tot Liab'ties	**14**	**14611**	**15177**	
Equity	15	10207	10112	

— INFRA UK —

If management's assumptions are correct, both profit and cash flow will reduce. If the Company's objective is to retain last year's return on capital of 49.93% management must ask the questions 'How much must volume/prices/material usage/production costs/numbers of employees/average earnings be varied to give a return on capital of 49.93%?'

Analysing the variables shows that 49.93% return on capital can be achieved if management's assumptions are correct and if the following changes can be made in operations:

- Volume is increased by 7.1% *or*
- Prices are raised by another 3% *or*
- Material usage is reduced by 5.1% *or*
- Production costs are reduced by 17.3% *or*
- 106 employees are dismissed *or*
- Average earnings per hour are reduced from £4.41 to £3.69.

It is not, of course, practicable to concentrate on one variable only. What would happen if there were a simultaneous improvement of 1% in each of the following?

- Volume
- Prices
- Materials usage
- Production costs
- Personnel employed
- Debtors (i.e. a 1% improvement in the time of collection)
- Inventory turnover (i.e. 1% reduction in inventory and WIP)

The new Profitability Tree shows that 1% was not quite enough. Still better performance is needed to achieve the 49.93% target for return on capital.

INFRA method
DSRM Budget 1986

1% improvement on key factors

PROFITABILITY TREE

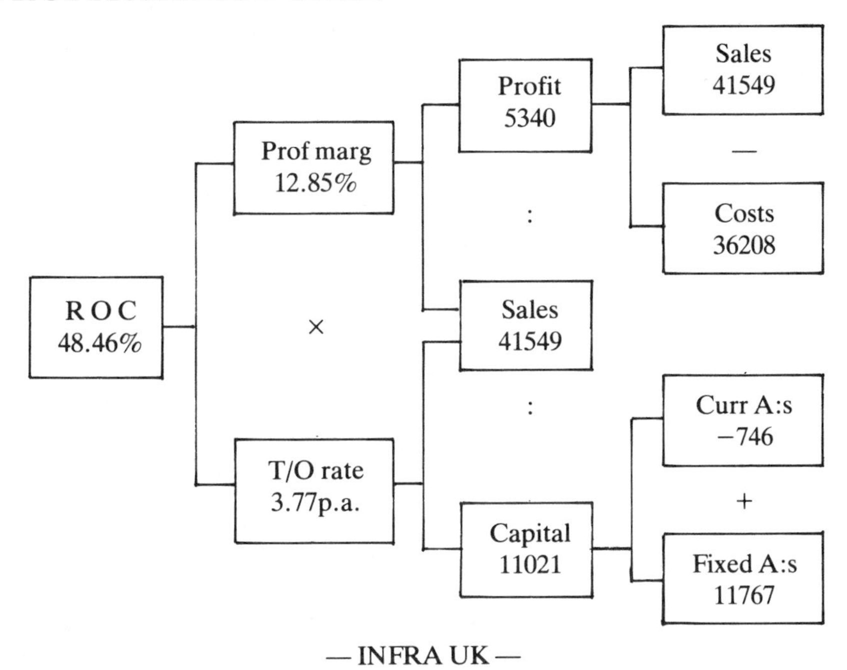

— INFRA UK —

A typical final question would be:

'Having improved 1% on all of the above items, how much more do prices have to be increased to restore last year's profitability?'

The answer is 'By another 0.4%'.

This short exercise shows how susceptible a business is to any of many different changes. It also shows what opportunities exist from quite small changes. If they complement each other, small improvements can add together to make big changes. If everyone in the company walks in the right direction, the results are much better than if they are all running but in different directions.

4 · Everybody can do better

In most sports 'dream limits' have been exceeded in recent years. A good example is the four minute mile which was considered by many to be beyond human achievement but which is now within the grasp of most good club athletes. Even more dramatically, the Olympic record for the male pole vault has risen from 4.38m in 1948 to 5.81m in 1984. Improved training methods, refined technique and better equipment (principally the glass fibre pole) have resulted in such improvements that we cannot see the limits to future achievement.

There have been similar advances in the world of business. No company can boast that it has no room for product development, organisational improvements, better methods or greater involvement and effort which will further improve results in quality, service or value for money.

To achieve the active and positive involvement of everybody in any firm all of the employees must know what is meant by high quality, good service or improved results. Anyone who is to be called upon to play a part in improving results must be able to see what effect his efforts have in order to be able to participate usefully in discussions, decisions and actions which will bring about an improvement.

A business must always be asking itself questions. In this chapter we will examine some of the questions which are typically asked, try to explain their significance and suggest how considering (and possibly answering) some of these questions can lead to improvements.

The questions which we will consider are:

- 'Are we doing what we should be doing?'
- 'How much do our products cost?'
- 'Are we pricing our products correctly?'
- 'What should be the level of our administration costs?'
- 'Are we making full use of the capital which we employ?'
- 'Is our investment policy correct?'

Fig. 9. The development towards better results seems to have no limit; either in sport or business.

What should we be doing and how are we doing it?

The well known management consultant, Peter Drucker, has produced a simple formula for success:

1. Do the right things

2. Do things right.

Above all, to do the right things is to produce and sell a product or service that customers want and are willing to pay for. Doing the wrong things can never be the best policy, even if you do those things in the right way.

Market Knowledge — the springboard for success

Companies have continually to ask themselves 'What range of goods and services should we offer?' The first stage in answering this question is to know the market. Who are our potential customers? What do they need? How do they use our products? Do they approve of our products? If so, why did they choose to buy from us rather than from our competitors? Without the answers to these questions we do not know which products to develop or how to market them.

The narrow sector

To decide what is the potential of a business, it is useful to define the factor or factors which limit the growth of added value. We call this the narrow sector. In some companies this may be skilled personnel. A profitable order may have to be turned away because there are not enough skilled welders available to complete the job on time. In another case the capacity of a particular machine may be the narrow sector which limits production. Most frequently, the market itself imposes the limits: staff and plant are available but the demand does not exist

In a bakery, if there is a demand for the goods, oven capacity is often the narrow sector. Let us assume that Big Baker makes three products. Party Bun, Dream Biscuit and Dainty Cake. There is one oven which is fully committed for the whole working day. If extra oven capacity was available the company could sell more of each product.

Profitability analysis

The bakery is operating at full capacity; the narrow sector is fully committed. The first step in any attempt to increase added value is to carry out a profitability analysis on the products. For this analysis we need certain information.

- Units sold of each product
- Price per unit
- Material cost per unit (raw materials, packing etc.)
- Time used in the narrow sector (the oven) per product
- Accessible oven capacity.

Production and sales for a normal month are given in the table below.

N.B. For simplicity we disregard all costs except the cost of materials. If we decide that the oven cannot operate for more than 220 hours per month the maximum added value on this product mix is £4,530.

		Per Unit			Total		
Product	Units	Price (£)	Mate-rial (£)	Added value (£)	Added value (£)	Hours in oven	Added value per hour in oven
Party Bun	5,600	1.10	0.80	0:30	1,680	80	21:00
Dream Biscuit	8,000	0.90	0.70	0:20	1,600	100	16:00
Dainty Cake	2,500	1.50	1:00	0:50	1,250	40	31:25
				Sum	4,530	220	20:60

The most important column in this profitability analysis is *'added value per oven hour'*. If all the eggs are put in one basket and only Dainty Cake which has the highest added value per oven hour was manufactured the figures would be:

		Per Unit			Total		
Product	Units	Price (£)	Mate-rial (£)	Added value (£)	Added value (£)	Hours in oven	Added value per hour in oven
Dainty Cake	13,750	1:50	1:00	0.50	6,875	220	31.25

As a result, added value has risen to £6,875 from £4,530. If 13,750 Dainty Cakes per month can be sold, added value can be increased by more than 50% without any investment. In reality, it is seldom possible to make such drastic quantity changes. The example does, however, show the range of possible strategies that can be revealed by profitability analysis. For example, if only 10,000 Dainty Cakes can be sold and Big Baker cannot use the full oven capacity he would still have an added value of £5,000 — 10% more than in the first analysis. If 10,000 Dainty Cakes can be sold there is a need to redistribute oven capacity among the different products so that the narrow sector (the oven) gives the maximum return.

WHAT DOES IT COST TO MAKE A PRODUCT?

Fixed and variable costs

Every car owner is sure to have asked himself 'What does it really cost to run my car?' If a neighbour wants to borrow it over the weekend at 'cost price', what should he pay? The very least that can be asked is that he should pay for the petrol and oil: consumption and cost per mile of both of which can easily be calculated. It is also reasonable for something to be paid for the wear and tear which will result. How is account taken of motor tax and insurance? These costs will be just the same whether the neighbour uses the car on one or on two occasions.

If the car were being loaned (hired) by a car rental business, the argument is changed and *all* the expenses must be covered, otherwise the business will run at a loss.

The question 'what does it cost to run the car for one mile?' is not easy to answer. The different expenses must be analysed and put into one of two main categories:

- Variable costs (those costs which vary depending upon the mileage travelled): petrol, oil, wear and tear.
- Fixed costs (those costs which remain the same whatever the mileage): tax, insurance, garage rent.

Variable costs (which the neighbour ought to pay when he borrows the car) can be expressed as pence per mile.

Fixed costs are normally expressed as £ per year.

Some costs are neither variable nor fixed. Depreciation is, for instance, primarily determined by the number of miles which the car has covered; but the second hand value also depends on the age of the car and falls every year, irrespective of the number of miles driven.

The distribution of fixed costs

The car rental business needs to fix its rates so that both variable and fixed costs are covered and to do this has to make an estimate of the miles that will be driven during the year. Dividing this figure into the total of fixed costs gives a figure to be charged for fixed costs per mile.

Variable plus fixed costs per mile equal total cost per mile and, if the firm is to break even, this is the least that a customer should pay.

This method of calculation has an in-built problem. The number of miles for which the car will be hired in a year has to be estimated. If the fixed costs (which are themselves an estimate, based in part on wear and tear, for an estimated number of miles) are deemed to be £1,200 p.a. and the estimated mileage is 40,000; the fixed cost per mile to be charged will be 3p; what happens if only 30,000 miles can be sold? The firm only gets 30,000 × 3p = £900 towards fixed costs. £300 less than estimated. Even allowing for a slight over-estimate for the wear and tear element in the total fixed costs, the cost of driving one mile will be higher than the original estimate.

Calculating the cost of making a product is at least as difficult as calculating the cost of running a car for one mile.

Fig. 10. Calculating the cost of making one unit of a product is at least as difficult as calculating the cost of running a car for one mile.

Manufacturing costs

Why is it so important to know the costs of manufacturing a product? There are two main reasons:

- Before fixing a price, the manufacturer needs to know his costs. Products should only be sold at a price below the cost of manufacture when there is a known and accepted reason (e.g. ousting competition) which justifies the practice and then only in the short term.
- Without a knowledge of manufacturing costs it is not possible to plan operations. The material, personnel and resources needed for a particular level of production need to be known to construct a business plan.

Pricing and planning are important business decisions.

Estimating and costing

Professionally, we speak of estimating when we calculate manufacturing cost beforehand and of costing when the calculation is made after manufacture.

Continuing with the example of the cost of running a car, we would say that an owner who has just bought a car can use the manufacturer's information to *estimate* fuel consumption. This estimate gives the anticipated consumption under *normal* conditions. It can be used to compile a budget of the first year's expense. By keeping a record of the petrol actually used and dividing this figure by the miles driven he can *cost* the petrol usage per mile. There will, invariably, be a difference between the estimate and the cost because of such departures from the normal as poor tuning, inconsistent driving, continual town driving etc. One or two fillings of petrol may not have been recorded which makes it appear as though the car is more economical than is really the case. The manufacturer's estimate may be rather optimistic. Whatever the reason, the variation is a *signal* that all is not as expected and that something has to be done.

If, after the first year's running has been costed, it is concluded that nothing out of the ordinary has occurred, these costs can be used as the *estimate* for the next year's budget.

What is variable and what is fixed?

There remains the question of 'what is the cost of manufacturing a product?' The most simple part of the calculation is deciding how much material and packing is needed. If accurate records have been kept of manufacturing methods it is possible to calculate roughly the man hours needed to make the product. From this the *direct labour cost* can be calculated. Material and direct labour costs are examples of *variable costs*: The larger the quantities manufactured, the bigger the total variable costs. But how variable are labour costs? If the factory is stopped for one day, employees are still paid. In fact, labour is a *semi-variable cost*.

By definition, fixed costs do not change in line with the volume of production — for example, factory rent and administration wages. If the volume of production is doubled, the factory will have to be enlarged and more administrative staff employed but the factory will not have to be doubled in size: nor will the administrative staff have to be doubled. Such costs must, therefore, be classed as costs which vary step by step and can be classified as *semi-fixed*.

The truth is that very few costs are either purely variable or purely fixed. The nearest one can get is to arrange cost items on a scale from very variable to very fixed, e.g.

Very variable — Sales commission
↑
Raw materials
Packing materials
Freight
Direct Labour
Electricity
Advertising
Testing Costs
Research and Development
Stationery
Telephone costs
Staff wages
↓
Rental charges
Very fixed — Audit Fees

This scale is not true for all businesses. In some companies electricity or telephone costs may depend directly on the volume of production or sales.

For practical costing purposes, the different cost items have to be categorised.

- Costs which are expressed as £ per unit will be called *variable*.
- Costs which are expressed as £ per year will be called *fixed*.

This is a gross over-simplification of reality but, considering that business administration is not an exact discipline, it constitutes an acceptable rule of thumb.

At this stage we must introduce the concept of marginal or contribution costing. This is the idea that once variable costs have been covered, any further income contributes towards fixed costs. Beyond that a full recovery of all costs (variable plus fixed) is necessary before the figure of invoiced sales (price multiplied by quantity) makes a *contribution to profit (CTP)*.

Calculating profitability

No method of calculation entirely replaces the need for judgment based on common sense. Nevertheless, a simple and realistic method can help to provide the basis for exercising judgment.

To take a practical illustration examine the three products of our bakery using annual rather than monthly figures:

		Per Unit			Annual Total	
Product	Units produced	Price (£)	Material Cost (£)	CTP (£)	CTP (£)	Oven used (hrs.)
Party Bun	67,200	1.10	0.80	0.30	20,160	960
Dream Biscuit	96,000	0.90	0.70	0.20	19,200	1,200
Dainty Cake	30,000	1.50	1.00	0.50	15,000	480

For simplicity, regard material as the only variable cost. All other costs are fixed and total £50,000 per annum.

It is easy to calculate the variable costs. For the Party Bun it is 67,200 × £0.80 = £53,760 per annum. But how are fixed costs to be allocated? The recommended method is to distribute fixed costs in the proportion that each product takes of the narrow sector: in this case, the oven. Out of 2,640 hours available in the oven, the Party Bun takes 960 hours — 36%. 36% of the fixed costs of £50,000 is £18,000. The key to the distribution of the fixed cost is the narrow sector.

			Variable costs				Fixed Cost	
Product	Units	Price (£)	Per Unit (£)	Total (£)	Distribution hours in oven	%	Total (£)	Per Unit (£)
Party Bun	67,200	1.10	0.80	53,760	960	36	18,000	0.27
Dream Biscuit	96,000	0.90	0.70	67,200	1,200	46	23,000	0.24
Dainty Cake	30,000	1.50	1.00	30,000	480	18	9,000	0.30
			Total	150,960	2,640	100	50,000	

Picking out the essential information from this table we get:

Product	Price (£)	Variable Costs (£)	CTP (£)	Fixed Costs	"Profit" (£)
Party Bun	1.10	0.80	0.30	0.27	0.03
Dream Biscuit	0.90	0.70	0.20	0.24	—0.04
Dainty Cake	1.50	1.00	0.50	0.30	0.20

In fact Dream Biscuit is being produced at a loss.One immediate reaction would be to discontinue Dream Biscuit production but would this be a sensible step to take? What happens if Dream Biscuit production ceases?

- 1,200 oven hours will be unused.
- Fixed costs will remain at £50,000.
- £19,200 of CTP will be lost.

By loading Dream Biscuit's share of the fixed costs on to the other products the profit of £4,360 will be changed to a loss of £14,840 unless use can be made of the 1,200 oven hours. It will only be the right decision to cease Dream Biscuit production if the oven hours made available can be used to produce a more profitable product i.e. one with a greater CTP. In the case of the bakery this could be done only if sales of Party Bun and Dainty Cake can be increased to take up the oven hours or a new product more profitable than Dream Biscuit can be introduced. There are many pitfalls in pricing and costing and, whatever figures are available, judgment is still needed to make the final decision.

In the case of the bakery, management would have to assess the probability of increasing sales of Party Bun and Dainty Cake and the cost and possible success of a new product against the known fact that Dream Biscuit produces a CTP which, whilst not covering the fixed costs allocated to that product, enables the bakery to operate at a profit.

WHAT IS THE 'RIGHT' PRICE?

Pricing is difficult

One of the most critical and difficult tasks for a business is accurate pricing of the goods or services which it offers. There are two standard methods — one or other of which is used in most cases.

1. Variable costs plus an allowance for fixed costs plus a desired profit = Selling price.
2. Market price (what the customer is willing to pay) — variable costs = CTP (fixed costs + profit).

The first method starts from total costs (variable + fixed) and from this one can calculate a price which the customer has to pay to cover these costs and yield a reasonable profit. This is the cost price method of calculation.

The second approach begins with a judgment as to what the customer will be prepared to pay. Taking the variable costs away from this assessed figure results in a contribution which, if the company is to be profitable, must cover both fixed costs and a profit element. This is the contribution method.

Both methods have advantages and disadvantages. Before assessing their value there are some fairly obvious propositions to be considered.

1. The value of a product to a customer depends on the benefit it gives him. The costs incurred by the manufacturer are of no concern to his customer.
2. The customer will continue to buy the product so long as the price does not exceed the value and unless he can buy the same product (or a satisfactory substitute) elsewhere at a lower price.
3. If the manufacturer is to stay in business, what his customers in total pay for the product bought must cover both variable and fixed costs and (preferably) yield a profit.

Fig. 11. The customer is only concerned about the benefit the product gives him. The manufacturer's costs does not interest him.

If the manufacturer uses the cost price method he may arrive at a price which is either more or less than the buyer would be prepared to pay. In the first place he loses the order; in the second he loses a possible profit.

Using the contribution method it is possible to fix prices at a level at which the excess over variable costs does not make a large enough contribution to cover fixed costs and an allowance for profit.

Calculations need to be supported by judgment.

Refer again to the example of the bakery. The price status of the Party Bun (as shown on page 75) is:

Selling Price	— £1.10 per bun
Variable Costs	— £0.80 per bun
CTP	— £0.30 per bun
Fixed Costs	— £0.27 per bun
'Profit'	— £0.03 per bun

If a customer offers to buy 1,000 Party Buns but only if we will give him a 10% discount (i.e. a price of £0.99 = £0.08 less than the total cost) the immediate reaction is to reject the order because it can only be met at a loss. But what if we have some spare oven capacity so that we can make 1,000 Party Buns without adding to the fixed costs? In that case by accepting the order we make a profit of £190 which would not otherwise have been made (Price £0.99 — variable cost £0.80 = £0.19 × 1,000 = £190). The correct decision cannot be made without a thorough knowledge of the market, the production capacity and the different elements of cost — what would have been the effect on the decision about the additional order for 1,000 Party Buns if it had involved extra heat in the oven, some overtime working or an additional transport charge?

Discount and mark-ups

Any discussion on pricing must include a consideration of the practice of offering discounts. Discounts are offered in an attempt to increase sales and, hopefully, the added value. Discounts should only be given when a full consideration of the market position has led to the conclusion that the extra volume sold will justify the lower income from each unit. How many more Party Buns must be sold to compensate for a discount of 10% on all sales? The answer is that anything less than a 58% increase in sales will result in a loss.

The opposite applies to mark-ups. The increased price can result in a reduced level of sales without affecting the profit. By increasing the price of the Party Bun by 10% we can lose nearly 25% of the numbers sold and still make the same added value as before.

Before deciding whether or not a price should be discounted or marked up, the basic facts need to be checked on:

Party Bun

	Selling Price £	Variable Costs (£)	CPT (£)	Units	Change in Volume	Total CTP
Now	1.10	0.80	0.30	67,200	—	20,160
10% Discount	0.99	0.80	0.19	106,105	+58%	20,160
10% Mark Up	1.21	0.80	0.41	49,170	−27%	20,160

Sound commercial judgment is the basis for reasonable pricing decisions.

Fig. 12. A discount must result in increased sales if a fall in profits is to be avoided.

The relationships between volume, price, capacity, market demand and profit are some of the most important issues in making business decisions.

What does 'overheads' mean?:

What is administration?

A large share of company expenses is covered by the word 'administration'. What exactly does it mean?

One way of grouping the tasks in a firm would be:

1. *Buying*. The purchase of all the goods and services needed for the conduct of operations.
2. *Adding Value*. The activity which turns the purchased goods and services into saleable products.
3. *Marketing*. Marketing and selling the finished goods.
4. *Commercial*. Invoicing goods and collecting accounts.
5. *Administration*. Collecting, processing and circulating information.

The first four ('primary') tasks are needed in any business, however large or small. They must be carried out if the organisation is to operate — even in a one-man business. When the business grows it becomes necessary to handle information so that the four primary activities can continue. Special staff, even whole departments, have to be recruited to carry out this process. The process is that of collecting information from outside and inside the firm and then analysing, processing and presenting the information in the form of:

- Plans
- Calculations
- Reports
- Designs
- Instructions

all of which are the products of administration. All of these administrative functions exist only to support and make more efficient the four primary functions.

Is 'administration' necessary?

The products of the administration process have a market inside the firm — the customers are the managers of the primary functions who need these products to carry out their own tasks. The difficulty is in evaluating the administrative products. The producers will always maintain that their products are needed but the real value can only be assessed by the user in response to such questions as:

- Did you know that this information existed?
- Have you a use for the information?
- Would your work be prejudiced if the information appeared less frequently?
- What would be the effect on your job if this administrative service did not exist at all?

This is simply a market research on the need for the products of administration. Bear in mind Peter Drucker's rule of 'doing the right things'. In any large company there are many cases of 'wrong things being done with great skill and expertise'. An unnecessary report accurately computed, elegantly detailed and produced at the speed of light is still unnecessary.

Fig. 13. In every large company there are examples of 'wrong things made the right way'. A typical example is the amount of unnecessary information produced by computers.

Eliminating costs that make little or no contribution to the primary functions can result in big savings; and can often be done without impeding those parts of the firm that generate earnings. Regular reviews of the administration activity are as necessary as regular weeding in a garden.

Parkinson's Law

Professor C. Northcote Parkinson is immortalised in business literature by his book 'Parkinson's Law'. When studying the employment statistics of the British Colonial Office he discovered that numbers of clerical staff employed over the 20 years from 1935 to 1955 could be summarised.

1935	**1939**	**1943**	**1947**	**1954**
372	450	817	1139	1661

Comparing these figures with the figures for physical area and population of British Colonies during this period, Parkinson discovered that in area and population there was little change between 1935 and 1939; a considerable reduction to 1943; an increase between 1943 and 1947 and, finally, a dramatic reduction as more and more colonies became independent. Nevertheless, the numbers employed continued to grow. Parkinson concluded that there is no connection between the volume of work and the number of clerical staff employed: in fact the number of clerks grew each year by 5.75% regardless of the organisation's output. According to Parkinson there are two factors which are to blame:

1. As part of his career pattern, every clerical officer tries to increase the number of his subordinates.

2. Clerical work by its nature creates more work for other clerks.

These are two of Parkinson's by now famous laws: another being that 'work expands to fill the time available'. In other words even the smallest and simplest task can be made so complicated that it keeps the staff fully employed in doing it — a feature which is not confined to white collar workers.

Parkinson's book sees work from a humorous angle but makes, most effectively, some very serious points about the ability of workers to beat 'the system', the potential savings (or capacity for extra production) which exist in any organisation and the need to be fully aware of the cost of labour — a most expensive element in most manufacturing, service or commercial organisations.

Capital employed — a hidden resource

The profitability of a business (i.e. the ratio between profit and the capital employed to make that profit) can be improved either by:

1. Increasing the level of profit.
2. Reducing the level of capital employed, or
3. A combination of the two.

The capital employed falls into two categories — working capital and fixed capital: the difference being that working capital is those assets which are in continual use and which are constantly changing in both form and value whereas fixed capital is in use over a considerable period of time; during which time its cost is amortised or written off as a charge on the business. Both types of capital tie up cash and reduce the profitability of the company if they are employed in excess of requirements. Cash flow (the availability of ready cash to meet immediate demands) has spelt the death of many firms. Turning unproductive assets into cash can mean the difference between survival and failure.

Where is working capital employed?

There are two main areas in which working capital is absorbed — inventory (including work in process) and debtors (people owing money to the firm).

The chain of operation is:

Supplies > Materials > Work in progress > Finished goods > Debtors > Cash

Inventory and W.I.P.

A look at Big Baker's accounts in chapter 2 shows that £770,000 (Inventory and W.I.P. £150,000:Debtors £620,000) is tied up in working capital. This is more than half of the capital employed of £1,100,000; a ratio which is not at all uncommon for manufacturing and trading companies.

Debtors

How can debtors be encouraged to pay more promptly? Some well proved methods of hastening payments include:

- Make sure that invoices go out as soon as the goods or services are supplied.
- Have a routine of monthly statements, payment reminders, follow up telephone calls and salesmen's calls which goes into action as soon as an account is overdue.
- Interest (details of which should be printed on the invoice) can be charged on overdue accounts.
- Discontinue deliveries until overdue accounts are paid.

Always be firm and consistent when applying your policy for debtors. You only need to consider your own methods in settling accounts to appreciate that suppliers who are active in pursuing their debtors are those who are paid first.

Creditors

The strict accounting definition of working capital is Current Assets minus Current Liabilities. Accordingly any delay in paying Creditors (the opposite side of the coin to encouraging Debtors to settle more promptly) is another way of decreasing working capital and maintaining a flow of cash.

Materials

Control of inventory and W.I.P. is the subject of contradictory requirements.

1. The desirability of being able to deliver from stock (a plentiful stock of finished goods) and not to be short of materials for manufacturing (a plentiful supply of raw materials): *against*
2. The need to reduce capital employed (small stocks).

The logistics of handling the flow of materials has been developed into a sophisticated science and many inventory and production control theories and models have been produced. These systems often require high levels of expertise and, sometimes expensive paper work or computing systems. They are usually appropriate for the large organisation but not justified in the smaller firm. In the firm which does not go to these levels of sophistication, simple methods carried out accurately and consistently can make considerable reductions in inventory without jeopardising deliveries of raw material stocks.

For example:

- Break each incoming order down into its raw material components and by a regular check on orders awaiting delivery be aware of raw material requirements.
- Insist on regular stock taking, simplified by using standard batch sizes, containers and unit quantities.
- Dispose of small items of uncalled for goods.
- Regularly review products and production methods to rationalise components.
- Balance discounts for bulk purchase against the cost of storage.
- Pursue an aggressive buying policy and insist on quick deliveries, thereby making suppliers hold stocks for you.

Systematic planning inside the firm can economise on material usage: the skill is in finding the position which most suits your requirements along the scale from:

(a) Planning by order — production does not start until there is a confirmed order from the customer e.g. bespoke tailoring.

(b) Planning by forecast — production begins without an order in anticipation of a forecast demand e.g. ice cream, perfumery.

Most firms have developed their own system and fall between the two extremes. The operations of a pizzeria could be demonstrated as in the diagram.

The pizza baker uses a combination of planning by order and planning by forecast. He makes 'semi-finished products' (dough, sauces, fillings etc.) based on forecasts. A pizza is not, however, made until there is an order. Imagine the situation if he used either planning method exclusively.

Planning by forecast would necessitate quantities of all 20 varieties of pizza being made in advance. The result would be an enormous quantity of finished pizzas (probably leading to over supply and wastage) and poorer quality for the customer because completed pizzas have been standing in stock.

Planning by order would mean that for each customer the whole process of making the pizza (dough, sauces, fillings etc.) would not start until the customer arrived. The result would be unacceptable waiting for the customer, over-crowding and confusion in both working areas and the shop or restaurant at busy times and very short production runs with excessive cleaning and washing-up times.

The situation adopted by the pizza baker gives an acceptable level of quality and service linked with low stock-holding. He has found the right point on the scale between planning by forecast and planning by order. Finding this point on the scale can be a great advantage to any manufacturer. In furniture manufacture it is common to manufacture the wooden carcasses by forecast and paint and assembly against actual orders. Even when making a product to a customer's specification (e.g. an architect-designed house) it is often possible to manufacture semi-finished components (window frames), sub-contract modules (kitchen fittings) and use standard materials (electrical wiring and plugs).

Fixed Capital

Over-investment or premature investment in fixed capital can leave the company short of cash in the same way as too much investment in working capital. An ill-judged investment in fixed capital can even result in a partial or complete loss of the funds which have been used.

How do we make the right investment decision?

Arriving at the optimum investment decision can be an impossible task however carefully we plan and forecast and whatever expertise is used. We read in the newspapers of firms which have gone into liquidation because they did not invest in new plant and machinery. We also read of firms which have gone into liquidation because they invested too much or at the wrong time. A willingness to invest is no guarantee of survival. Investing wrongly can be worse than no investment at all.

Making precisely the right investment is an unenviable task. By hindsight we can say whether or not an investment has been successful just as we know the result of a football match after the game. Whether the investment was successful or unsuccessful can depend upon factors that could not have been foreseen — market fluctuations, government policy, the emergence of a substitute for your product, an overseas competitor willing to buy his way into the market. An obvious example of the risk attached to investment decisions is the effect of the oil price rises in the late 1970s on many European companies. Making accurate investment forecasts is as difficult as making accurate long-range weather forecasts.

Long-term investments

Some capital acquisitions can commit the business forward for long periods of time, can tie up enormous quantities of cash and can determine the future of the business. For example:

- a shipping company ordering a new super tanker
- a paper mill buying a new paper making machine
- a wholesaler building a new distribution centre
- a shipyard building a dry dock
- a steel manufacturer opening a new rolling mill.

Fig. 15. These idle supertankers are examples of 'wrong decisions made the right way'!

Such acquisitions *must* be successful and highly proficient companies go to great lengths (hiring experts, appointing special committees, making computer simulations) to help them with the decision. Notwithstanding, there are many idle super tankers, abandoned steel works and paper mills running at half capacity. The purchases were 'right' when the decisions were made but went 'wrong' because of events that had not been (possibly could not have been) foreseen. As Peter Drucker says 'if a company does the wrong thing it is of no help to do it the right way', with modern equipment, sophisticated methods and skilled personnel.

Even small capital purchases need careful consideration

If the company is basically doing the right things in the right way there can be many opportunities to improve by comparatively small acquisitions — a new truck, a computer installation, an automatic lathe.

Such acquisitions are not as important as the major items but they need careful consideration and should only be undertaken if they can be seen to improve the company's potential profitability. To make a purchase merely because an item of equipment is x years old, because a new model is available or to be in fashion is not a good decision. Before investing the project must be evaluated by asking the questions:

- What will be the cost?
- What additional earnings will the purchase yield or what savings will it make?
- When will the expenditure and earnings or savings occur?

In the accounts only tangible things are classified as *acquisitions* — property, machinery, equipment. Money spent on marketing, research and development and training are classified as *costs*. We must always remember that such costs have to guarantee improvements leading to increased profitability if they are to be justified. There is no fundamental difference between paying £100,000 for a machine and spending the same sum on a training programme or a research project. In both cases, the objective is to achieve better results in the future.

An example

Assume that production capacity at Darlington & Simpson Rolling Mills Ltd (DSRM) — the firm featured in chapter 3 — will not meet customers' demands.

A decision is taken to expand capacity by 10% in volume. The relevant figures are:

- Cost of acquisitions: £3,000,000.
- Additional annual operating and maintenance expenses: £450,000.
- Additional labour = 30 persons.
- Estimated life of equipment: 10 years.

The project is being financed by:

- A bank loan of £1,500,000 at 15% interest.
- £1,500,000 taken from earnings and cash in hand.

Is this likely to be a profitable project? One guide would be to consider the effect of such an investment on the 1985 figures (see page 56) assuming that the project had commenced at the beginning of the financial year and had resulted in a 10% increase in invoiced sales. By feeding these figures into the computer, we come up with the following results:

Investment programme

INFRA method
DSRM Actual 1985

	LINE	£000	£/H	
Invoiced Sales	1	42670	30.87	Added Value
Materials etc	2	21336	15.43	
Production Costs	3	6982	5.05	
Added Value	**4**	**14353**	**10.38**	
Wages & Salaries	5	5651	4.09	Distribution of Added Value
Employment Costs	6	909	0.66	
Corporate Taxes	7	2545	1.84	
Interest	8	297	0.21	
Dividends	9	1678	1.21	
To Int Parties	10	11081	8.02	
Left in Business	**11**	**3272**	**2.37**	

Incr Creditors	12	0	0.00	Funds Statement
Decr Debtors	13	0	0.00	
Incr Other Debts	14	5344	3.87	
Decr Other Crs	15	0	0.00	
Ext Financing	16	5344	3.87	
Cash at Disposal	**17**	**8616**	**6.23**	
Acquisitions	18	4960	3.59	
Incr Debtors	19	1665	1.20	
Decr Creditors	20	384	0.28	
Change Inventory	21	2259	1.63	
Incr Other Crs	22	316	0.23	
Decr Other Debts	23	0	0.00	
Tot Expenditurs	**24**	**9584**	**6.93**	
Change in Cash	**25**	**—968**	**—0.70**	
Profit Bef Depr	26	7792	5.64	Profit & Loss Account
Depreciations	27	1480	1.07	
Profit Aft Depr	28	6313	4.57	
Profit Bef Tax	**29**	**6015**	**4.35**	
Corporate Taxes	30	2545	1.84	
Net Profit	32	3470	2.51	
Capital Employed	33	15683		Ratios
Turnover Rate	34	2.72		
Profit Margin	25	15.08		
Return on Capit	**36**	**41.03**		
Equity	37	10880		
Return on Equity	38	55.28		
Equity Ratio	**39**	**39.55**		

	LINE	OPENING	CLOSING	
Cash in Hand	1	1663	695	Balance Sheet
Debtors	2	5291	6956	
Inventory, WIP	3	3306	5565	
Other Credits	4	292	608	
Fixed Assets	5	10207	15167	
Depreciations	6	0	1480	
F.A. Book Value	7	10207	13687	
Total Assets	**8**	**20759**	**27511**	
Creditors	9	6548	6164	
Current Account	10	218	83	
Bank Loans etc	11	800	2300	
Borrowing Need	12	0	0	
Other Debts	13	4105	8084	
Tot Liab'ties	**14**	**11671**	**16631**	
Equity	15	9088	10880	

— INFRA UK —

INFRA method
DSRM Actual 1985

Investment programme

PROFITABILITY TREE

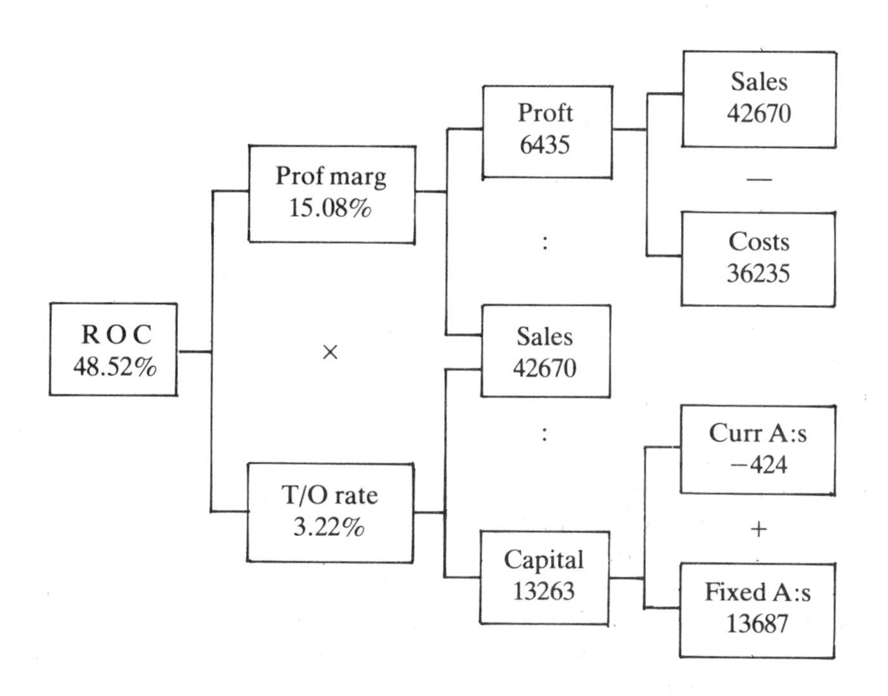

CASH FLOW

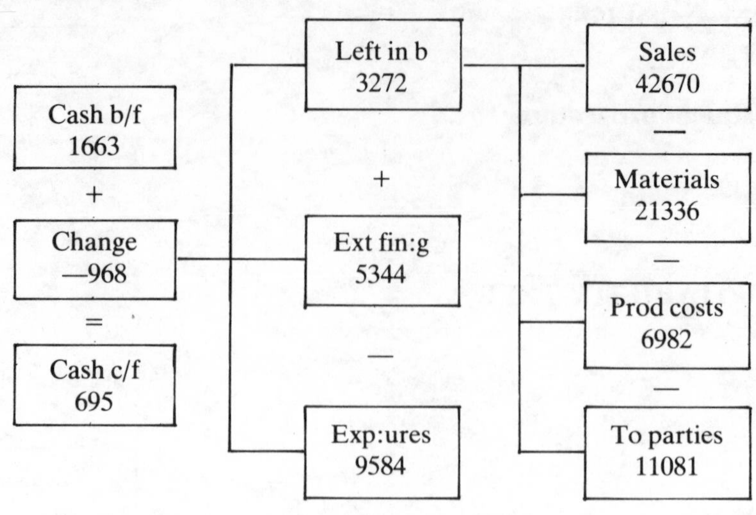

Borrowing need: 0

— INFRA UK —

Before considering the results the readers must appreciate that the finance needed is not limited to the acquisition of fixed assets. The working capital (debtors and stocks) has also to be increased as volume increases.

The indications are that this would be a profitable project. Even though Return on Capital Employed falls from the actual 49.93% to 48.52% the investment programme adds £673,000 to the company's profits before tax. Added value per hour also increases from £9.74 to £10.38, despite the inclusion of some 60,000 more hours.

At first sight this is a sound project but, before making a final decision, safety margins have to be considered. Things can go wrong and often do at the least favourable time. What would be the result if all of the following adverse happenings occurred?

- No growth in sales volume.
- Prices have to be reduced by 2% to avoid a positive fall in sales volume.
- Operating and maintenance costs increase by a further £200,000.

The impact on the business would be:

- Return on Capital Employed falls to 30%.
- Profits before tax fall to £2,800,000 — a reduction of almost 50%.
- Added Value per hour falls by 15% to £8.27.
- There will be a negative cash flow of more than £3,000,000 — necessitating a further bank borrowing of £1,600,000.

The example serves to prove how difficult it can be to achieve the right investment decisions. If customers fail to respond as anticipated the project could lead to disaster. On the other hand, in a competitive market, it could be disastrous *not* to undertake the project, without which market share and profits could fall during the years to come. Making precisely the right investment decisions is a well nigh impossible task.

In attempts to make investment decisions less risky, the accountancy profession has devised means of illustrating movements of cash more vividly and developed techniques, (such as discounted cash flow) which allow for variations in the value of money — inflation or deflation. Similarly marketing experts have produced techniques for evaluating likely market responses (e.g. the use of surveys and opinion polls). These techniques provide a greater volume of more accurate and more easily understood information but they do not remove the need to exercise commercial judgment when making the final decision. For small firms, in particular, these techniques can involve proportionately large outlays of money although, if they result in the right decision, this can be money well spent.

5 · The reality of planning

So far we have been considering the current performance of a business: what the numerical and financial information tell us about the way in which the firm is conducting its affairs: whether or not it is operating successfully.

It is equally important to think about the future. What needs to be done to survive tomorrow? The security of the firm and the jobs of the people who work in it depend upon accurate forward planning. The more the employees understand of what is being planned for the future, the more likely it is that the plans will be accepted and worked for as a team; with a consequent greater probability of satisfactory results.

This chapter will be concerned with plans, budgets and systems of monitoring and control.

'Navigare Necesse Est'

In Scandinavia one of the highlights of the sailing year is the 24 Hour Race. Yacht owners make careful preparations for this event. Equipment is renewed, repaired and checked thoroughly; crews train themselves for sailing and navigating through the night; essential spares, stores and provisions are taken on board and stowed.

The rules of the race are quite simple. The objective is to sail as far as possible and to return to the starting point within 24 hours. The result is measured in nautical miles travelled (1 nautical mile equals 1,852 metres). There are several different starting points and a number of turning points round which the yacht can sail; but you cannot double the same turning point more than twice. Each yacht skipper chooses his own route and turning points. Late arrival is punished by a substantial deduction in the number of miles credited. The scale of these deductions is such that it usually does not pay to arrive late, even though you have chosen a route that gives extra mileage.

A well prepared craft will arrive at the chosen start point in good time. The boat is fully equipped; all of the necessary spares are on board; compass, log and radio are functioning properly; stores and provisions are on board; the crew is well trained and accustomed to working together.

Before starting, a rough plan is made of the proposed route; taking account of the prevailing conditions and the weather forecast. This is the first stage of planning and includes a detailed plan for the first three or four hours sailing. No attempt is made to plan the whole route in detail; a change in the wind can mean that everything has to be re-calculated.

What we have is a general picture of the total plan and a detailed plan for the first stage. It is also advisable to have alternative plans to meet likely eventualities 'if the wind goes into the NW when we round the Alma should we head for x instead of y?'

What is a realistic objective for this venture? We dare not hope to win our class. Our aim is to beat our own previous best of 95 nautical miles; 100 miles would be very satisfactory. That means we must average 4.2 knots and gives us some targets for the first stage: 'we aim to round the Alma shoal before midnight'.

From the start everything goes smoothly. The log shows a speed of 5 knots — nicely above our required speed. After 4 hours, 18 nautical miles have been covered — an average speed of 4.5 knots. Now is the time to plan the next four hours.

The result of the '24 Hours' depends on a number of factors — the yacht, its equipment, the crew, the skill of the captain. It also depends on the weather. All of the crews have the same information at the start (Wind: NW 8-12 m/sec) but if after 12 hours the wind turns to (Wind: W 15 m/sec) a radical change of plan is needed to reach the goal of 100 nautical miles in 24 hours.

Managing a company is like sailing in a race

In many ways managing a company is like competing in the '24 Hours'. The boat corresponds to the production plant, the crew to the employees and the captain to the management. The weather report is like the economic forecasts made by banks, business institutes and economic forecasters.

The critical difference is that this kind of sailing is a leisure activity undertaken for pleasure whereas management is all about earning a living for everybody in the firm. Company results are not measured in miles, but in economic terms, as we saw in Chapter 2.

In planning for the business future, there are certain terms which are in regular use.

Forecast: An estimate of future happenings and economic conditions that will affect our operations but are not likely to be affected by what we do.

Operational Plan: A description of the measures that we will take.

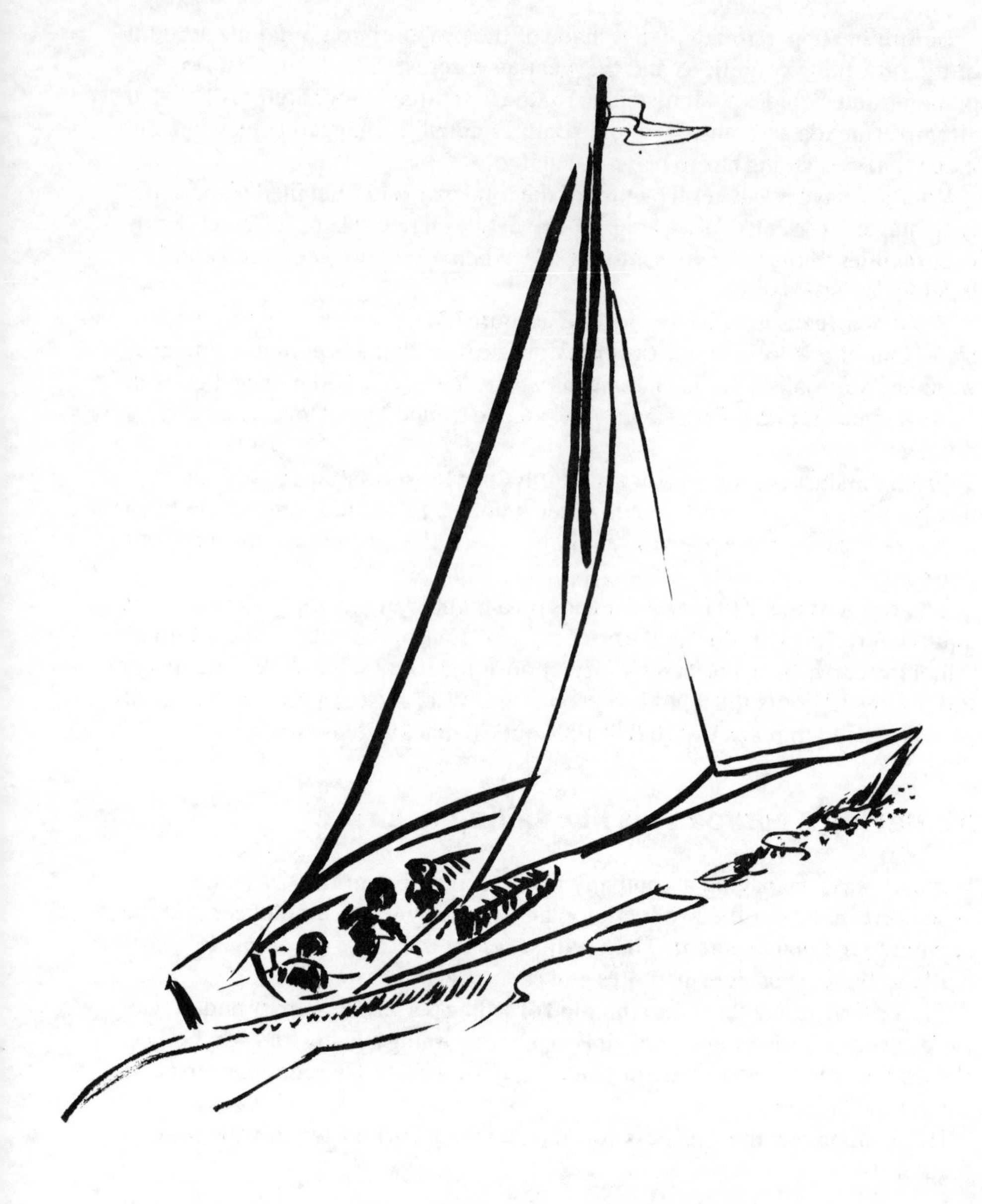

Fig. 16. In many ways managing a business is like sailing.

Resource Plan: A calculation of the resources (plant, equipment, personnel) that will be needed to realise our operational plans.

Budget: The estimated economic consequences of the action which we plan.

Outcome: The actual results as compared with the forecasts, plans and budgets.

Example

The weekend will be warm and sunny (Forecast). I will go swimming (Operational Plan). I need a bathing costumer (Resource Plan). I expect it will cost about £7.50 (Budget). It actually cost £10 and it was cold and wet all weekend (Outcome).

Planning — thinking in advance

Planning is looking into the future. Anticipating happenings which will affect our business. The most important function in business is to be able accurately to estimate the economic consequences of different alternatives and to make the decisions to do today what is necessary for us to survive and prosper tomorrow.

Strategic Planning

The firm exists in a world in which it is surrounded by customers, suppliers, competitors, local and central government bodies, national and international trade movements. This environment is in a state of continuous change. To survive, the company must adapt its policies and activities to the changes which are taking place. This adaptation takes time; sometimes a long time. Therefore the company needs a 'radar system' which will monitor the changes which are taking place all around and indicate the changes needed inside the business for the firm to compete and survive. This is the task of strategic planning.

As a lode star we have the basic function of the business: those customer needs which the firm is qualified to satisfy. We have to recognise the relationship between *needs* and *means*. The *need* to remove beards has existed for very many years and, for most men, will presumably continue into the future. The *means*, however, have changed from the cut throat razor to the safety razor and then the electric shaver. A firm which was in business in the 19th century to make cut throat razors will have disappeared. But if the business function was to 'meet the need of removing beards' there is a good chance that the firm is still alive and prospering.

Fig. 17. Human *needs* do not change as quickly as the *means* by which they are filled.

Another example is that for many years ladies wore stockings held up by suspenders. The introduction of pantihose or tights drove out of business those manufacturers who could not adapt quickly enough. The fashion for pantihose was the death knell for these firms. But for the firms which had an active radar system and appreciated the effect of the coming of the mini-skirt there was a perfect business opportunity. Winston Churchill was quite right when he said that 'Most threats are possibilities in disguise'.

One of history's most famous enterprises, Columbus's discovery of America, was a complete planning failure. He ended up as far from his real goal (the East Indies) as was possible. A modern bureaucratic organisation would probably have fired him for ineffective planning. However, we all know of the possibilities revealed by this setback.

Fig. 18. Columbus's discovery of America was a complete planning failure.

Strategic planning has to answer questions about the firm's future such as:

What are the needs of the customer?

How will these needs change?

What customer needs can be most effectively met from our resources?

How should we develop our resources to meet the customer's future needs?

What should we manufacture ourselves and what should we sub-contract?

What do our competitors do and what are they likely to do in the future?

How much planning should we do?

In recent years there have been several planning 'doctrines' ranging from an almost superstitious belief in the effectiveness of total planning to almost a complete denial of any need to plan.

The two factors which principally determine the extent and detail of a company's forward plan are:

1. The market situation and particularly the stability of the market.
2. The ability of the business to adapt to changing conditions — its flexibility.

Taking these two factors together we have a planning matrix

Market / Flexibility	Stable	Unstable
High	Undertaker	Fashion shop
Low	Water Purification plant	Car manufacture

This describes a range of planning situations.

Undertaker — A stable market which can be forecast. Few technical innovations. No heavy fixed assets. Little need for planning.

Purification Plant — Market changes very slowly and will not produce surprises. Equipment is complex and expensive. Technical changes require careful long-term planning. Little need for market planning: considerable need for technical planning.

Fashion Shop — Very capricious and unstable market. A high degree of flexibility; styles and models can be changed in a few months. Not much need for planning but must be able and willing to react quickly to a changing situation.

Car Manufacturer — The worst of both worlds. The market is unstable — very sensitive to changes in the overall economy and subject to international competition. The industry is not very flexible — a new model needs up to ten years for development with enormous changes in machinery and methods, with the result that reorganising the production process is lengthy and expensive. Many of the business disasters of the 70s and 80s fall into this category of an inflexible industry in an unstable market — steel mills, shipyards, car manufacturers.

The need for flexibility

The turbulent international economy of the past decade has emphasised the need for flexibility and many firms have tried to reduce the complexity and ponderous nature of their operations. One method has been by concentrating on the core business with which the firm is involved and buying in the ancillary activities. Specialist companies deal in transport, printing, cleaning, translating, training etc. Each business should concentrate on those activities in which it specialises and which it performs well. A computer manufacturer with all its own resources in the ancillary fields mentioned above would reduce its flexibility considerably. A decision to introduce a new style of print out could have to wait until the printing works had been re-equipped.

If all of the ancillary activities come from outside suppliers, the company can concentrate its managerial and technical skills on the core business in which it is highly proficient. By switching between suppliers, the company can maximise flexibility and it is often very much cheaper to buy in the activities. The rate per hour of activity may seem high but specialising leads to efficiency, bad work is not paid for and when the specialist services are not in use they do not cost a penny, instead of comprising a permanent overhead cost.

'The planner is always wrong'

We often hear this opinion voiced by businessmen. Whenever materials or labour are in short or over-abundant supply, the planner is blamed. The task is not an easy one: principally because of the speed with which market conditions can change. He has the same problem as the skipper in the '24 Hour' race who planned on a forecast of a North Westerly wind of 8-12 metres per second but faced a reality of a Westerly wind of 15 metres per second. In its own way planning is a form of adding value by transforming raw market information into detailed plans which can be used to initiate day by day operations.

Another 'flow' can now be added to the cash flow model. The flow is called the 'process of planning' and consists of a flow of *information*.

Forecasts and operational plans lead to resource planning which in turn leads to the acquisition of resources — manpower, materials, machinery. These in turn generate expenses which eventually, we hope, result in an inflow of cash from customers who have been supplied.

Getting this flow of information to function properly is one of the industry's biggest and most difficult problems and the malfunction of the information flow is at the root of many business difficulties. Some of the most frequent problems are:

1. Poor forecasting. Customers do not behave in the way anticipated. Customer behaviour is basic to all operations and a failure to forecast accurately leads to problems in all of the subsequent processes.

2. Poor communications and lack of co-operation between design, sales and production departments, because they do not understand each other's problems.

3. Changes in the market discovered too late in the day.

4. Planning procedures which are too slow and cumbersome. The system reacts too slowly to change.

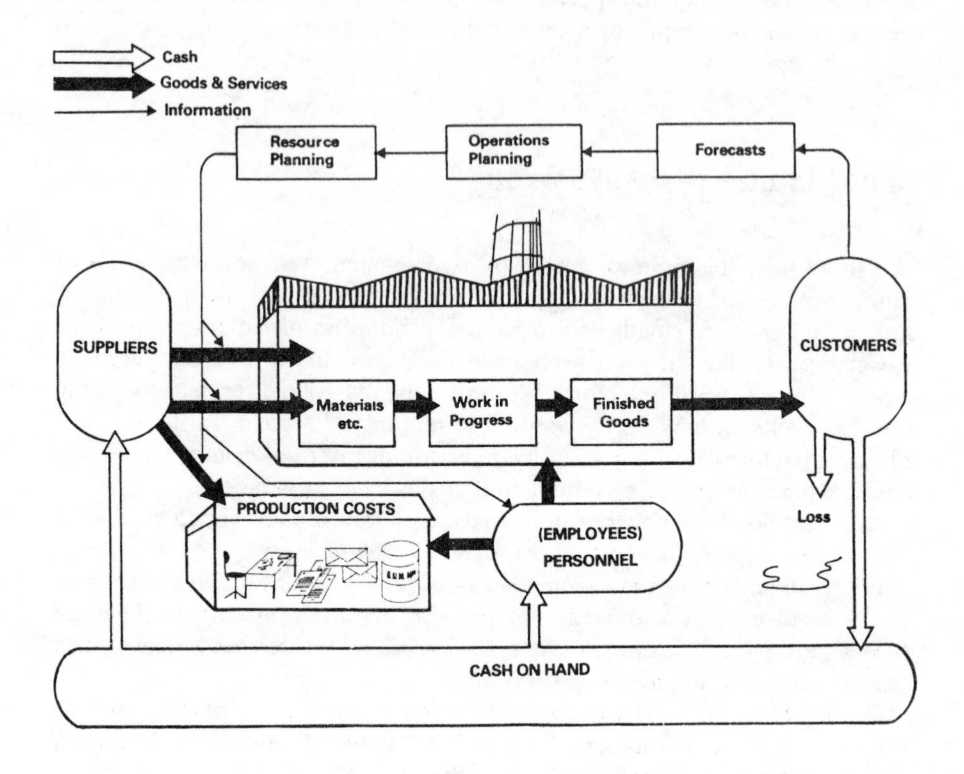

Planning departments are not always wrong in their calculations. Most business failures occur because customers, over whom we have no control, act in a way which had not been anticipated.

Fig. 19. Many planning failures are caused by factors outside the company.

The forecast, or estimate, as a basis for planning

The operational plan for the bakery might be:

Party Bun	67,200 units
Dream Biscuit	96,000 units
Dainty Cake	30,000 units

What do we need to know to produce a *resource plan*, giving the manpower, machines and raw materials that are needed? The basic information document is the recipe which is simply an estimate stating how much work, raw material etc. is needed under normal conditions.

For good planning reliable and realistic estimates are needed and it is important to monitor actual performance and analyse the variations between the estimate and the outcome. A typical estimate could be:

Product: Party Bun

Batch size: 100 units

Raw materials

		£
Flour	8.82 kg at £0.43 p kg	3.80
Yeast	0.15 kg at £1.25 p kg	0.19
Margarine	0.26 kg at £1.50 p kg	0.39
Miscellaneous		0.02
		4.40

Labour

0.6 hours at £6 p hour	3.60
Total variable costs	£8.00

Fixed Costs* (hours in oven as base)

1.43 hrs at £1.89 p hour	£2.70
Cost price	£10.70

*The method of calculating fixed costs is that used in the previous example on page 75.

This provides a sound basis for resource planning. To make 67,200 Party Buns (672 batches of 100 units) the following are needed:

Raw Materials (£4.40 × 672)	£2,956.80
Man hours (0.6 × 672)	403
Oven hours (1.43 × 672)	960

Monitoring can be done in one of several different ways. One is by sampling. Walk into the bakery and check the amount of flour being used to make a batch of 100 units. Another way is by measuring the total consumption over a month and comparing this with the estimated consumption.

For example:

	Actual production	Flour used. Estimate p 100 units	Estimated consumption
Party Bun	5,600 units	8.8 kg	493 kgs
Dream Biscuit	8,000 units	8.6 kg	688 kgs
Dainty Cake	2,500 units	10.2 kg	255 kgs
			1,436 kgs

1,436 kgs is the estimated consumption. Checking the delivery notes from the flour mill reveals that 1,620 kgs have been delivered. What is the reason for the discrepancy? There is a difference of 184 kgs (value £79.12). Where did it go? Some possible explanations are:

- Purchases exceeded actual usage. In consequence the stock of flour has increased. This can easily be checked if we have the figures of stock (inventory) at the beginning and the end of the month.
- The bakers are not keeping accurately to the recipe and each bun is slightly heavier than estimated.
- It is not possible to keep to the recipe in present conditions, in which case it is time to change the recipe.
- One or two batches have been burnt in the oven and thrown away. This is waste and if we know that it will happen and what percentage of production is involved we can take it into account in the costings.
- Careless handling has resulted in broken bags and spillage on the floor. This is another kind of waste at the raw material stage.
- A short delivery by the supplier was not noticed and the delivery note has not been amended.

Except for the first (increase in stock or inventory) all of these variations result in *losses* for the firm. Management has the job of finding out what the fault was and taking appropriate action.

Manpower planning

At first sight estimating manpower requirements is no more difficult than that for materials. The estimate says Manpower 0.6 hours at £6 p hour = £3.60 for a batch of 100 units.

But, what kind of hours? Whose hours? The estimate says that it takes a professional baker 0.6 hours (36 minutes) to bake 100 buns. This implies that he works steadily for 36 minutes without interruptions. Left alone to work for a full 8 hour day he wili bake more than 1,300 buns. This is not reality! In the course of a day there will be all sorts of disturbances and interruptions — material too hard, machinery breakdowns etc. He also has other things to do as well as making buns — cleaning, rest periods, training, union meetings etc. These factors make it difficult to plan personnel activities. It is not enough to know that a professional baker bakes 100 buns in 36 minutes if free from interruption. It is also necessary to know:

1. On average how much of a normal day is used for production?

2. What allowance needs to be made for absence (sickness, etc.)?

Without this information it is not possible to calculate the number of full time bakers who will be needed in the coming year.

Let us take an example. In a typical bakery approximately 6 hours in every 8 are available for production. The rest is used for cleaning, waiting for materials etc. — this we call *indirect* time. Out of the 220 working days in the year each baker is absent on average for 20 days. A normal working year looks like this:

Vacation	25 days			
Absence	20 days	=	160 hours	
Indirect time	50 days	=	400 hours	Presence
Production	150 days	=	1,200 hours available	
Total			1,760 hours available	

To calculate the number of bakers needed to produce 67,200 buns (672 batches of 100):

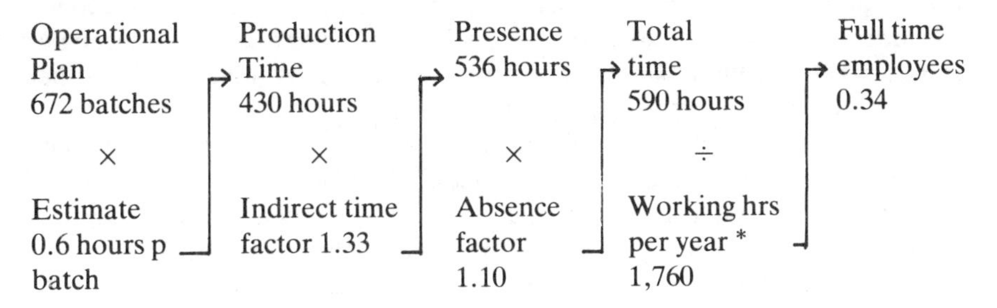

*Normal working time for a full time employee without absence.

Complete a similar calculation for every product and by adding the 'Full time employees' figure from each calculation we arrive at the total number of bakers needed to staff the bakery. This figure is only correct if:

- the operational plan is correct; which can only be the case if the *forecasts* are accurate
- the labour *estimate* is realistic, which infers that all of the bakers are fully competent and work at a normal speed
- the *estimate* of indirect time is correct. Indirect time can easily increase if there are frequent raw material shortages or machinery breakdowns
- the estimate of *absence* is correct. This is very difficult to estimate and can vary with all sorts of things over which the firm has no control. A recent example has been the effect of Self-Certification of Sickness on absence statistics in the U.K.

It is most unlikely that all of these items will be correct, but this does not mean that it is not worth trying to make a plan. The plan may never be precisely accurate but without it there is liable to be either a shortage or an excess of manpower.

We can be fairly certain of two things about an operational plan:

1. The actual outcome will not coincide with the planned outcome.
2. Despite the discrepancy, the operational results will not be as bad as if no plan had been attempted.

Increasing productivity

A much debated and frequently misunderstood concept is that of *productivity*. One measure of productivity in the bakery is the number of buns produced per hours worked. In the example above it is the number of buns produced per hours of presence 67,200 ÷ 536 = 125 buns per hour.

It is often thought that increased productivity is the same as increased speed of operation. This is a complete misunderstanding of the real nature of productivity, although speed of operation has an effect on the numbers produced at least in the short term. The issue of speed of production is not entirely irrelevant but increased productivity is not just increased speed of work.

Comparing the tons produced per working hour in today's steel mills with those at the turn of the century shows an astonishing increase in productivity. The same applies to paper mills and saw mills; sometimes as much as a tenfold increase. If these increases arose purely from increases in the pace of work either the workers of today are running around like the workers in Chaplin's film 'Modern Times' or the workers of the 19th century moved like sleepwalkers. There is no doubt that people worked hard at the turn of the century and that sheer speed of work cannot possibly be the main reason for the scale of recent increases in productivity.

Real increases in productivity can, in the long run, only be achieved by:

- Improvements in raw materials. Better raw materials result in improved products and easier methods of manufacture.

- Better and faster production plant.

- Improved methods which make it possible to increase production with the same effort.

- Better management practices eliminating disturbances, waiting time and unnecessary work.

- Improvements in manufacturing plant which enable greater quantities to be made by fewer workers.

The best way to increase productivity is by stimulating ideas and suggestions which affect these items and turning these ideas into improvements which change the job. Without changes in the job there will never be long run substantial increases in productivity.

Fig. 20. Increased productivity is not necessarily the same thing as increased pace.

The Infra method uses its own ratio to express an overall measure of productivity; that of added value per hour. The formula is:

$$\frac{\text{Sales — (Material + Production Costs)}}{\text{Hours worked}} = \text{AV per hour}$$

The inclusion of hours worked in the formula means that speed of work has an impact on the productivity index.

Productivity improvement does not arise from one factor such as the intensity of work. It owes far more to making more valuable products, economising in materials, saving on overheads, improving work organisation and being generally open minded to the concept of changing the job.

Budgeting

If a firm intends to make improvements of this nature it has to plan its financial progress. This financial planning document is the firm's budget. It is not unusual for people to ask — why spend time and effort in compiling a budget? Especially in large firms, budgeting is seen as being a painful nuisance. The budget department asks for a lot of detailed information about future prospects — information that the supplier does not need for himself. The only obvious reason for collecting budget information is to satisfy the ambitions of the accountants and the planning managers.

Looking at budgeting in this way is to miss the whole purpose of the budget. The budget information should not be just for the accountants and planning managers: it should be used by those responsible for achieving results.

Fig. 21. Budgeting is sometimes looked on as being the baby of over ambitious accountants.

When a family man asks himself 'If I buy this car and do not get a rise in wages, how much will I have left each month for food and clothing?' he has, in fact, compiled a budget. He has calculated the *economic consequences of an action*. If the amount left each month for food and clothing is insufficient, he will have to postpone buying the car. Alternatively, he could construct a different budget by buying a cheaper car or getting a better job.

The purpose of a budget is to estimate beforehand the economic consequences of different courses of action. From these it is possible to choose the alternative that gives the best return.

Chapter 3 has an example of a budget which shows the vulnerable areas as well as the opportunities of the business. The example chosen was from a company in a strong financial position. In most companies *cash flow* is the weak point of the business.

The best trained athlete will die in a few minutes if he loses a lot of blood. Cash is the blood of a business and cash flow the circulation system. A business

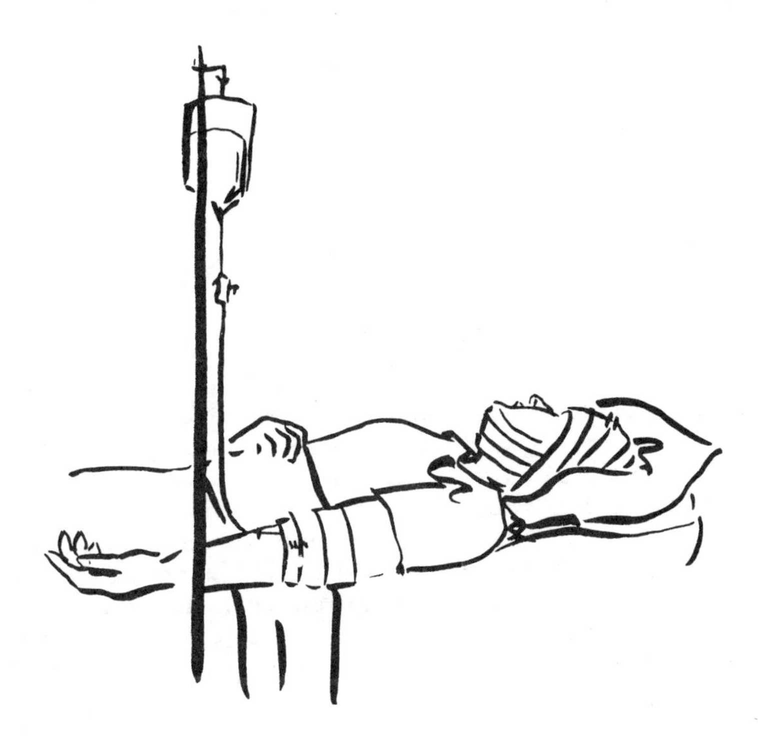

Fig. 22. Even a well-trained athlete cannot survive a severe loss of blood. In a business the equivalent of blood is **cash flow.**

can survive for a short time without profit if it has a positive cash flow. On the other hand, if it is short of cash it can go under with a full order book and working at full capacity. The planning and control of cash flow is increasingly an important task of management.

The exercise in Chapter 3 shows cash flow for a whole year; it does not give the situation for each month. Sometimes the bulk of acquisitions might be made at the beginning of the year, when sales are low; resulting in a negative cash flow. In fact a monthly, or at least a quarterly cash flow forecast is desirable which also includes such items as value added tax, National Insurance contributions and employers' tax contributions.

It is good policy to keep in touch with the bank and produce a budget. Banks are usually well disposed towards clients who present a detailed budget and cash flow. The firm which gets short shrift is the one that comes running to the bank at the last minute when the cash has run out asking for a promise of extra credit or the postponement of a repayment date.

As part of the function of keeping an eye on the business it is necessary to follow up and thus to see how closely the firm adheres to the planning and budget documents.

FOLLOW UP

The means of navigating the business

Consider again the '24 Hour' race. After 4 hours, the position had been checked and it was found that 18 nautical miles had been covered at an average speed of 4.5 knots. That was more than the 4.2 knots needed to achieve the objective of 100 miles in 24 hours.

This is an example of a follow up report; a report which says exactly where the firm is and which can be compared with the budget; the document which says where the firm ought to be. This comparison points the way forward.

These are the instruments needed to navigate a ship. In business the instruments for navigation are forecasts, estimates and reports. The captain of the yacht has the right to know at least:

- that he is given an accurate position
- that the position is given when it is needed and not when the next stage has been started on

- that there is a means of comparing the actual position with the intended position to give a check on progress.

Comparable information should be available to the management of a business.

Some common imperfections

Some of the most common weaknesses in business reporting systems are:

Unreliable basic data. A report can never be better than the input data on which it is based. The information about hours worked and material used is usually supplied by people outside the accounting department where the budgets are calculated. The information suppliers usually do not know why this information is needed or how it is used. They may not see the output report. In such cases, it is not surprising if poor input data is supplied. It is, therefore, advisable for those who provide the input data to know the reasons why the report is needed, as well as to see the final report.

Reports which are too bulky. If a report contains too much information, the reader will either only read parts of the report or gloss over the essential points. Compare it with the daily newspaper. A paper printing all of the news reports and bulletins unabbreviated and unedited would not be read. An edited version of the most important news is what is needed.

Reports which are too difficult to read. This is another field in which the businessman can learn from the journalist. Like an article in a paper, a report should be easy to read and should emphasise the essential points. Diagrams and graphs often make the point more successfully than columns of figures. *Reporting by exception* is one way of emphasising the essential by only reporting the facts which are unanticipated or differ from the normal. A good comparison is the oil warning light on a car. The 'budget' for normal oil pressure is fed into the system which reacts by showing a coloured light only when the pressure goes below the desired level.

Reports coming in too late. The requirements of completeness and accuracy often conflict with the need to produce the report when it is needed. An approximate report on time is often better than an exact report delivered too late. It is better to be vaguely right than accurately wrong!!

Incompatible information. The report must be in the same terms as those in the budget, in order to make comparisons. Unnecessary difficulties arise if the budget uses kilometres and the report gives distances in miles. Another common problem is to have related income and expenditure not connected with each other. For example: the budget for the first quarter contains details of an advertising campaign which is completed on time, the invoice for which is not registered until the second quarter. If the discrepancy is not noticed it could lead to the wrong conclusions.

A system which is too sophisticated and too expensive. Many a company has been persuaded by a skilled salesman to buy a computer system which has a capacity and features far beyond the firm's needs. This is like the orienteer who replaced his magnetic compass with a satellite navigation system. He would get accurate directions but he would need electric power and a parabolic antenna with him. As a result he would probably get stuck in the woods with his equipment and never reach his destination.

The follow up report lets the firm know where it is. Accurate forecasts, good operational and resource plans and competent budgets are not enough without a reliable reporting system which will help the firm to navigate towards its destination of profitable operations.

6 · Working together for success

The more people there are in the firm who have the chance to share information, understand what it means and become involved in the economics of the business, the more smoothly and rapidly the firm will progress. The whole purpose of the INFRA method as described in this book is to help people to become involved and to make sure that everyone in the firm shares knowledge, insights and commitment to profitable operations.

Using the INFRA method in varying degrees, companies and units (ranging in size from 15 to 3,500 employees) have made progress with a measurable positive effect on the firm's success. Four companies, ranging from 30 to 400 employees and from metal-working to catering, have been chosen as illustrative case studies. All of these firms have two things in common:

1. Progress has resulted from close co-operation between management and employees. By using their knowledge of the company and its activities as seen from the grass roots level, by making suggestions, by working together to improve productivity, the employees have contributed towards the success of the company and can take credit for improved results.
2. In each case there has been some form of reward for improved results in which all have shared. The INFRA method makes possible the establishment of quick, accurate, realistic and easily understandable methods of measuring results. Not only can these measurements be used to calculate rewards, they also provide information which adds further to an understanding of how 'our business' works. The more people understand, the more willing they are to make further contributions to improvements.

The metal components industry

The firm in question employed 30 persons, half of them white collar workers. The operation was partly manufacturing and partly wholesaling; selling technical components to the building trade for construction and repair work. Some of the items were bought in and others manufactured by the firm.

For some years management had been trying to involve the staff in running the firm by sharing information through a Productivity Committee. The members of this committee became well informed and felt involved but neither information nor enthusiasm was spread across the company.

One method was by publishing the year end results on the notice board in the following form.

	1977 £000's	
Sales	+705	
Raw materials, consumable stores		−291
Wages and salaries		−270
Overheads		−109
Interest payments		− 5
Depreciation		− 21
Taxation		− 3
Profit after taxation	+ 6	
Dividends	0	
Available for investment	6	

This presentation had much in common with an early INFRA table.

Beginning in 1979 the company presented its results by concentrating on one key unit of measurement defined in this way. From sales, deduct raw material and consumable store costs and what the firm called affectable costs (but not wages and salaries). The figure remaining is referred to as value added. By dividing this figure by the total of hours worked, we establish the key-figure of 'value added per hour'.

Using this method the 1977 figures would have read

	£000s	
Sales	+705	
Raw materials, consumable supplies		−291
Other affectable costs		− 55
Value added	359	
Working hours	42,118 hours	
Value added per working hour	£8.55	

This form of measurement corresponds with one of the INFRA key figures (added value, line 4).

Value added per working hour became the company target figure for each succeeding year. 1978, with a value added per hour of £9.07, was taken as the base year for future calculations.

In 1979 an agreement was made for all the employees — white and blue collar. This agreement established a bonus based on the va/h figure (a total sum of money) to be shared between all employees at the year end. The individual amounts were calculated according to each person's working hours during the year.

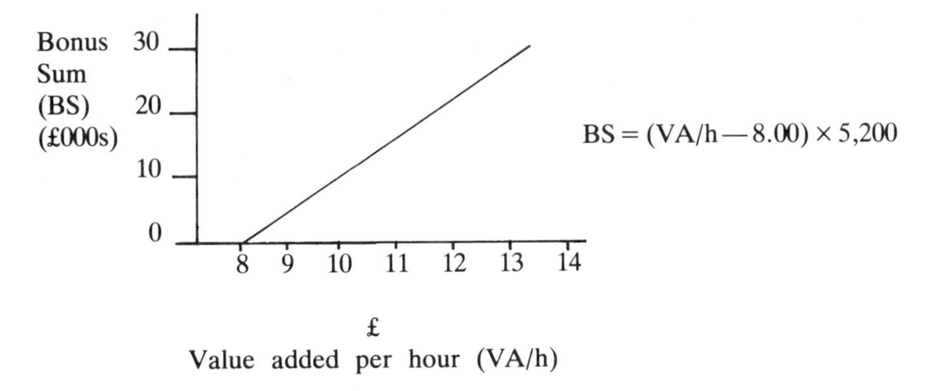

For a value added per hour figure of £10.2 the total Bonus Sum would be £ (10.2 — 8.0) × 5200 = 2.2 × 5200 = £11,440.

The data needed to calculate the value added per hour figure could be assembled quickly and the result published a few days after the end of each month. As a result the annual performance could be followed monthly and employees could answer for themselves such questions as

- 'How are we getting on?'
- 'What is the value added per hour figure so far?'
- 'What is the probable Bonus Sum for the year going to be?'

The published figures, the monthly results and the subsequent discussions became a lively and increasingly important element in the life of the company. The outcome was greater involvement, higher productivity and better financial results.

In 1979 va/h was £10.52 an increase of 16% over 1978. The 1980 figure was £13.00, a further 23% increase. An investigation in 1980 showed that productivity had increased by 30% since 1978. The increase, between 1978 and 1980 of £3.93 in va/h also meant more profit for the company, even after allowing for the bonus to employees. In 1980 the employees shared a Bonus Sum of £26,000 — equal to £0.51 per working hour.

The bonus agreement is adjusted each year to allow for inflation — an essential adjustment in this type of scheme. The solution adopted was to move the 'bonus line' upwards on the value added scale in proportion to the rise in the published index of inflation.

Since 1980 the results and the bonus have gone both up and down. Since 1981, like all other firms in the construction industry, the firm has suffered from the building depression. However, as the President said in his company newsletter, the firm coped more successfully than most of their competitors.

In periods when the bonus fell, people were naturally disappointed but there was no resentment and no demands for compensation — everybody knew the reasons why! They knew the reasons because of the firm's adventurous approach to educating and informing the work force. The agreement includes a system of information for all employees. Every month the figures used to calculate the value added per hour are made known. Sales, raw material costs, costs of supplies, 'affectable costs' and working hours. The va/h for this month and also for the year to date are given and the President also adds such comments as:

1. What is the month's figure? Is it good or bad? Why is it as it is? What divergencies are there from normal and why?
2. The effect on the Bonus Sum so far this year. 'Congratulations' or 'I am sorry!'
3. What does the future hold? What favourable or unfavourable indications are there? What needs to be done in the coming month to achieve good results, an improved va/h and a satisfactory Bonus Sum?'

This regular routine of information passing has contributed towards active involvement throughout each year. Points for consideration, suggested improvements and justified criticism are presented to management. The result has been a remarkable increase in productivity.

The important and, some might say, unusual features of the scheme are:

1. The monthly presentation of information to everyone in the company. Everyone has a continual interest in company performance.
2. Although monthly figures are produced, the Bonus Sum is calculated annually. This takes care of minor variations between months. If there is a Bonus Sum to pay at the end of the year, management knows that it has been earned by all the employees.
3. Everybody, irrespective of his job, gets an equal share of the Bonus Sum per hour worked. The system is designed to stimulate co-operation and to be a reward for results achieved by working together. An individual's performance is reflected in his personal salary.

The Chemicals Factory

The company employs 45 people in a process industry manufacturing chemicals for the plastics industry.

Typically for a process plant, there are high costs for converting from one product to another. 30% of the available time is spent in down-time preparing for another type of production. In addition, quality requirements are high; the cleaning down associated with changing product is particularly important and the process has to be closely controlled.

This company is a living proof of the fallacy of the statement that 'In a process industry the efforts of the employees have little effect on final results!' There is an element of truth in the statement if we think only of the production output whilst the plant is running as it was designed to run. But we also have to consider avoidable down-time, minor faults in operation, usage of material, level of quality, energy consumption and so on. Even in a process industry the employees' involvement and application have a decisive effect on efficiency and results.

During 1980 this company entered into a programme to promote efficiency in collaboration with all the employees. One part of this project was to find quantifiable productivity criteria which were reliable and could show the progress of the company in a way which could easily be understood. The criteria which appeared to be essential were:

1. *Invoiced Sales* which depend on the utilisation of plant capacity, the product quality and the pricing policy.
2. *Raw material consumption* which made up 55% of the total production costs.
3. *Working time* of all employees.

Routines for keeping records of all these criteria were well established. New administrative systems for follow-up reports were not needed. The new requirement was to gather up all this information into one system of measurement that could be understood by everybody.

$$\frac{\text{Invoiced Sales — Raw Material}}{\text{Worked Hours}} = \text{Resultant £/hour}$$

It was seen to be particularly important that this produced a unified measurement reflecting the results of everybody's efforts — blue collar workers, white collar workers, supervisors and management. Everyone can affect this figure, and, consequently, all working time is included below the line in the formula.

The resulting figure in the autumn of 1980 was £15.5 p hour. It was agreed that any improvement in this figure should give an extra profit for the company and also additional income for the employees.

An agreement was made on the basis of:

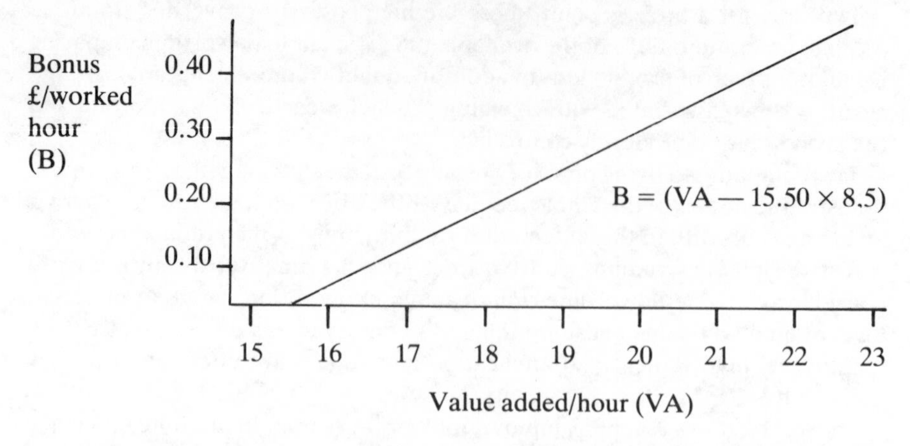

The company salesmen were also included in the scheme but their bonus was based on a factor of 15 instead of 8.5. This weighting on the sales bonus was to emphasise the importance of profitability to the sales force, instead of paying commission based on turnover which is the traditional way of calculating salesmen's bonuses.

It was agreed that bonus should be paid out twice each year: in June and in December. That would mean extra money, on top of ordinary wages, salaries and holiday pay, for the summer holiday and for Christmas.

If interest and commitment is to be maintained, results need to be reported more frequently than half-yearly. Results are, therefore, published each month and the bonus for an employee who has worked all his available hours is given. The actual bonus for each individual is accumulated and paid out half yearly.

The scheme began in the autumn of 1980 and everyone co-operated on the programme to improve efficiency. By as early as the first half of 1981 the average result had increased to £18.50 per hour. Each employee received about £220 before the summer holiday. The result for the second half of 1981 was £18.00 per hour and rather more than £170 was paid out to everyone at Christmas. During 1982 the figure was nearly £20 per hour. The efficiency programme, the measuring of results, the monthly information system and the bonus scheme have between them contributed to a dramatic improvement in results: raising the hourly figure from £15.50 in 1980 to £20 in 1982 (almost a 30% improvement).

The improvement is even more remarkable when one considers that it was achieved during a very depressing period in the firm's history. Whilst the bonus scheme was coming into operation raw material consumption by the plastics industry fell by about 30%. Company turnover fell from £3 million to £2.8 million but, most unusual for such a situation, they maintained profitability. The plant was located near a big city. Retirements and people leaving for other jobs were frequent. The employees remaining regularly succeeded in absorbing the work of employees who left. In this way during the first year of the bonus scheme the work force was reduced by 7 employees with corresponding bonus increases for those remaining who took over their work. The 1980/81 budget forecast the cost of labour at 8.3% of turnover. In fact it came out at 7.4%; the opposite of what usually happens in times of falling sales.

Raw material wastage fell from 6.5% to 4.7% — a saving of £26,000 per year. Absenteeism fell from 21% to 11% for blue collar workers and from 6.9% to 4.5% for white collar workers.

Management and union representatives agree that the commitment to higher productivity has led to an improved climate of co-operation and a better understanding among the employees of the conditions necessary for an improvement in company results.

The Hotel and Restaurant Business

An investigation into the Scandinavian hotel and restaurant business in 1978 predicted falling profitability and a decreasing market. Companies were accused of not being progressive and forward-looking and it was said that 'traditional organisation of jobs within establishments has contributed to keeping methods of operation that should have been changed in order to keep costs down. The variety of wage systems among restaurant personnel make it difficult to reform working methods'.

It has been traditional in Scandinavia for waiters to be paid on 'piece work'. The figure of '13% Service' at the foot of the bill is the waiter's wage. The greater the value of the meals he serves, the more he earns.

It is, therefore, the decision as to how the tables are shared out in a restaurant where there is more than one waiter which is important, because the distribution of tables affects the opportunity to earn a higher wage. Serving outside one's own tables means depriving colleagues of the chance to earn. The waiter's reply 'This is not my table' is not an attempt to put the customer in his place; it is a direct effect of this system of piece-work payment. It may not be easy for the customer to understand but it makes very good sense among the staff.

Fig. 24. 'This is not my table'
The method of payment often decides how the work is organised.

The method of organising work and the payment system have established a real constraint — lack of flexibility. Staff do not help each other in the ways necessary to run the establishment most efficiently. When the restaurant is quiet and the kitchen is busy, a waitress will not go into the kitchen to help. She is paid only to wait at table. Later when it is quiet in the kitchen and busy in the restaurant, no one comes to help the waitress because there is no way in which they can benefit because of the system of service charges.

Such constraints are not confined to restaurants; they exist in all types of industrial, commercial and service organisations. The result is a lack of flexibility, between different jobs, different kinds of labour, different levels in the work structure. An increase in flexibility between jobs is often the way to increased efficiency as well as enriching the jobs for the employees by offering more variety.

In the company concerned, which employs about 100, an investigation was carried out, in which both employees and management co-operated, to find solutions to the problems of organising the work.

One important point recognised was the need to sort out the wages system as a preparation for better co-operation. Instead of a few people (waiters) working on 'piece work' and everyone else on a fixed wage a common pattern for wages was wanted, so that all could contribute equally and share in the rewards. Success for the company depended upon better team work between the departments. Food, entertainment, accommodation and conference facilities had to adapt to each other and present a common front to provide a range of services for potential customers.

The crucial point of the different wage systems was sorted out so that all staff received personal monthly salaries. In addition a method of measuring the total results was created by using the formula:

$$\frac{\text{Turnover} — (\text{Raw Material} + \text{Wages} + \text{Salaries})}{\text{Worked Hours}} = £/\text{hour}$$

This was first tested out in the second half of 1979. The resulting figure was £2.50/hour after wages had been paid. This was not considered to be a satisfactory result. The aim of the project was to create a new system of job and work routines to achieve better results, to produce more money in which everyone could share. An agreement was made with all the employees resulting in an extra bonus, equal for all; by using the following formula:

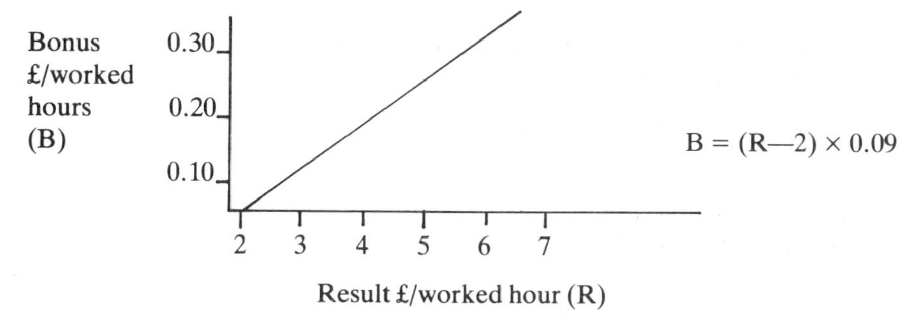

For the same period a year later the result was £4.30/hour. Subsequent calculations were not comparable because the firm invested in a building programme to provide more accommodation. The results formula was amended by moving the bonus line to B = (R—6) × 0.09.

The result was a much greater commitment throughout the firm towards the success of the company. Motivation, flexibility between jobs and willingness to help each other increased dramatically when the opportunities were apparent. All of the staff worked for the company as a team. 'This is not my table' is a phrase that is no longer heard in the company.

Loosen the handbrake and put it in gear

The new pay system dealt with a critical problem in the reorganisation. Further action was needed to move the business forward. The first step had loosened the handbrake. It was time to put it into gear. Particularly important steps in the project were:

1. A total reorganisation. This involved dividing the company into results units; each department having its own sales budget, cost budget, goals and targets. A procedure which measured departmental results combined with a wages system based on total company results proved to be a successful combination.

2. A computer-operated serving system was installed, by means of which communications between the kitchen and the restaurant staff is carried out by terminals and printers. The distance which the staff have to walk has been reduced by 50%. Restaurant staff can now spend more of their time with their customers.

3. Reviews have been made by the staff of working conditions.

4. Suggestions were collected from all members of staff; particularly in planning for the new building.

5. Team work, flexibility, training and education were discussed during the reviews and improvements were suggested.

6. Decision making and control of work were decentralised. Jobs were examined to clarify the responsibilities of the relationships between supervisors and their staff.

7. A written policy was devised for:

   - Long-term planning
   - Product development
   - Budgeting
   - Purchasing

- Recruitment
- Staffing
- Employment conditions
- Wages and salaries
- Training and education
- Maintenance
- Quality
- Marketing
- Public relations
- Co-operation between results units

8. Co-operation and co-determination at work were discussed with union representatives. Principles were laid down for dealing with:

   - The future policy of the business
   - Working conditions
   - Suggestions scheme
   - Departmental co-operation

9. Procedures for co-determination were incorporated into the company's organisation. Employee representatives were elected to the Board of Directors and the management team. Representatives were also chosen for each department. Since 1979 there has been no need for any special organisation for solving work problems.

10. Finally mention must be made of the fact that 33 projects suggested by employees were adopted and put successfully into operation.

This example shows that defining a joint bonus, measurement and information system is sometimes only a way to loosen the handbrake. In such cases, further steps are needed to carry the operation further. Once the employees see the need for improvement they want to become actively involved. It then becomes necessary to create and develop ideas and encourage activities so that positive commitment does not end in disappointment.

The Paper Mill

The company employed 400 people in a pulp-mill and a paper-mill. About 50% of the pulp is processed in the paper-mill and then finished in a paper-factory. As usual in this industry the firm works shifts round the clock. Many members of staff never meet at work. The company also has a repair and maintenance department and an administration department.

The project began as a wage-system project. The intention was to develop a procedure for measuring the most important indicators of performance for each department, leading to a consideration of a new wage system for the company. The project was carried out in close co-operation with the union representatives.

The result of the project on measurement was that two overall result measurements were developed for each of the production units and in turn further overall result measurements were developed for the whole company. The repair and maintenance and administration departments could not have their departmental results measured but were considered to be able to affect the overall company results. A model of the solution was:

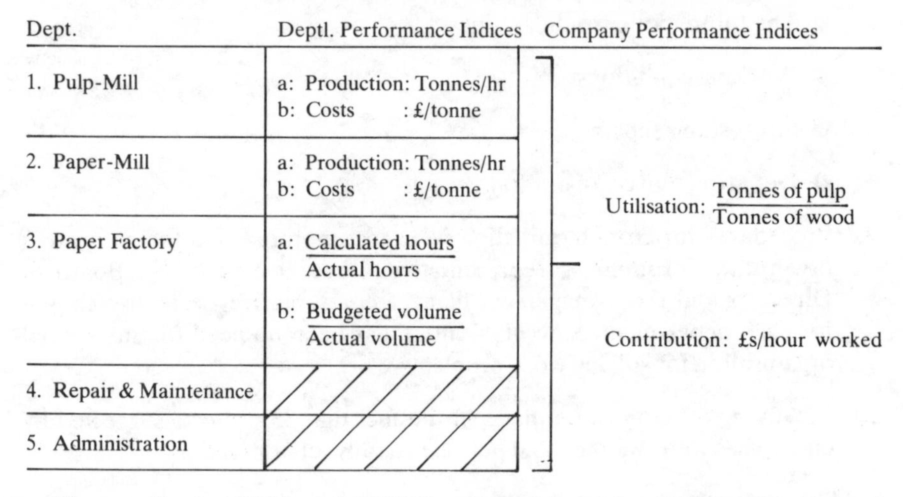

Dept.	Deptl. Performance Indices	Company Performance Indices
1. Pulp-Mill	a: Production: Tonnes/hr b: Costs : £/tonne	Utilisation: Tonnes of pulp / Tonnes of wood Contribution: £s/hour worked
2. Paper-Mill	a: Production: Tonnes/hr b: Costs : £/tonne	
3. Paper Factory	a: Calculated hours / Actual hours b: Budgeted volume / Actual volume	
4. Repair & Maintenance		
5. Administration		

The results for 1979 and 1980 were considered carefully. Reasons and consequences were discussed and, as discussions went on, the mutual dependence between departments became apparent. For example, increased throughput in the pulp-mill resulting in poor quality would make for problems in the paper-mill. Cost saving in one department could mean a cost increase elsewhere.

The company operates a continuous process. The path to better results is through better co-operation between the different operations in the process. Because energy is such an important cost factor, production interruptions in one department can result in energy costs elsewhere unless information is passed quickly from one department to another.

It was agreed that a bonus system based on departmental results would not be feasible. It would merely encourage everyone to make his own department profitable; possibly to the detriment of the firm as a whole. Common goals needed to be discussed and the overall measure of £/working hour was agreed upon as being the most suitable.

At the same time it was agreed that the overall figure was not enough for providing working departmental information which would show how their department had contributed to the overall results. This led to the conclusion that two systems were needed.

1. An information system whereby departmental results are presented monthly.

2. A measurement system to show the overall company result. This figure to be such that it could be used as a basis for calculating a bonus.

It is important to notice the procedures that were followed in order to achieve the necessary results.

- An agreement was reached with the unions. As a result people were encouraged to participate in the investigations and the changes necessary.

- Joint decisions were made about the procedures to be undertaken. A committee was set up with two blue collar representatives, two white collar representatives and two management representatives. This committee has the task of studying and commenting to all employees on the figures which are produced. The committee also collates employee suggestions and puts forward ideas to the management.

- The work schedule was radically revised to year round production. This increased the number of shifts per year, allowing the firm to make economies by planning forward the repair and maintenance schedules.

All of these activities, the system of bonus payment and the methods of keeping employees fully informed were drawn together into a Productivity Agreement.

The bonus system as defined above is based on 'operating profit before depreciation' or 'contribution III' as it was called in the company's ordinary profit and loss account. The results are calculated every month in cumulative 4 month rolling periods, a method which avoids too wide variations.

It is interesting to observe how 'operating profit before depreciation' or 'contribution III' (previously a strange and unimportant accounting figure) became important and understandable, uniting the whole company in consideration of a simple figure. It is worth noting that it is the discussions and increased knowledge arising from considering the figures produced which has created the involvement leading to a flow of creative ideas and suggestions for improvements.

The formula for the bonus system is

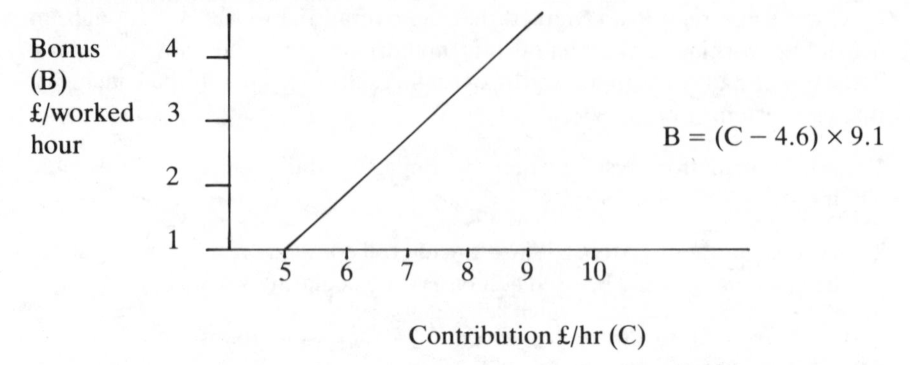

Contribution £/hr (C)

The productivity agreement and the work of the Productivity Committee demonstrated to customers, suppliers, bankers and others that those working in the company were prepared to work together in such a way that the company would be a good one with which to be associated. As a result, the company's operating base looks much more secure than when the agreement was signed in November 1981.

One example of the effect of this kind of venture is a document (originally hand written) from a foreman and his work team to the Productivity Committee. It is entitled:

Cost savings in the preparation department during December 1981

The report shows two major savings arising from the work of the team:

1. Saving of £1,700 in material usage.
2. Oil savings of £13,489 by reducing steam usage.

The report ends with:

Value of material saved on pulp production	£ 1,700
Reduction in steam usage	£13,489
Total of savings	£15,189

The body of the report is a list of eight points that the foreman has drawn up and hung on the wall of the plant. The list shows how to save on materials, energy and so on. At every point there is a calculation showing in cash what things actually cost. It is designed as a savings list in terms of £/hour or £/ton in steam costs. The list shows what will be the results if the team can improve production costs by concentrating on these eight points.

This project shows that you cannot specify the best size of a team for the members to work together. 400 people working on shifts make a big and diverse team. But the team work which is necessary is decided by the nature of the process. In a continuous process each section depends upon another, regardless of how many are in each work group. To achieve satisfactory results the whole work force must work as a team.

The project shows that management's dream of 'responsibility for results' and 'cost consciousness' can be achieved by providing simple measurements and presentations of figures which can be easily understood.

Co-operation for success

There are many examples of how a common enemy has united a group of people. It could be a nation at war or a company in crisis. What is needed is a focus — everyone knowing who or what is the enemy.

Today no jobs are absolutely secure. There have been many examples of big and previously successful companies which have had to reduce staff and even discontinue operations. The threat to jobs is the common 'enemy'. That was the case in all four of our examples. The inspiration in all of these companies was the realisation by both management and workers that jobs were in danger and could only be saved by close co-operation.

The realisation is based on a common view of financing jobs, seen from the viewpoint of job security as a positive objective. The INFRA method was fundamental in achieving this common point of view.

The main objectives are the development and continuance of jobs. But these must be good jobs. A good job is one in which the worker can see how his performance develops and how he contributes to the success of the company. The INFRA method has been used to provide this information.

It is apparent from the four examples in this chapter that increased productivity and better results do not necessarily mean increased stress and dissatisfaction with the job. On the contrary, job satisfaction is developed when work is better organised and when hold-ups and delays have been eliminated. More productive jobs usually correspond with more pleasant jobs and heightened job satisfaction.

There is nothing so satisfying as working together with others to achieve success.